The Beginning of the End of Racism in America

~ BLACK AND WHITE ~

Elaine Sharp and Richard Sharp Jr.

PAGE PUBLISHING, INC.
New York, NY

First originally published by Page Publishing, Inc. 2017

ISBN 978-1-64138-218-2 (Paperback)
ISBN 978-1-64138-219-9 (Digital)

Book cover conceptualized by Richard Sharp Jr.

Printed in the United States of America

Contents

Acknowledgments

I would like to acknowledge and give special thanks to my beloved parents, Elaine Sharp and Richard Sharp Sr., who have done a great job in raising me up in spirit and truth. Without their tender love, support, and guidance, this peace provoking book wouldn't be possible.

I would also like to give a special thanks to all of the loyalists in my life who aren't my mother and father, yet and still, they have been a solid foundation for me during these sixteen plus years of captivity I've had to endure. Thank you, Joe Bishop—my greatest friend and brother ever. My sister Zina Sharp—I love you, Princess Warrior! You are the greatest! Anthony Herd—you are a strong brother and a great brother-in-law. Keep up the good work! Teresa Mitchell—I love you so much! Thank you for everything, beloved! Karen Graham—you are still one of the nicest people in the world. Thanks for the love and support! To my siblings Gravinia Gipson, Carl Gipson, and Larry Gipson—I love you all so much, and I look forward to making many new memories with you all while we simultaneously treat our mother like the divine queen that she is and give her the life that she always wanted.

To all of my family and loved ones—Larry Smith, Willie Smith Jr., Aunt Georgette Kari, Uncle Walter, Aunt Loretta, cousins Tijuana, Phoebe, Bryan, Teresa, Pooh, Michael, Doug, Damien, Richard, Dorothy, John, James, Ernie, Wannie, Dreco, Mama, Sherisa, Brighty, Edwina, Jane, Jimmy, and to all cousins I don't know or have forgotten, I love you all, and I wish you all the best.

To Keonna Lynk, Leonna Jones, Deonna Lynk, Tijuana Lynk, Tammy, Kimmy, Gerrode, Sydney, Steffani, Tamika, Lil Rock, Shantana, Deneen, Maurice, Kim and Happy, K. T. Selena, my honorary son Cantrell Holmes, Crystal, Shirley, Melisa Kazlauskas, Tiffany Greenwood, Monique, E-Work, Belinda, Nita, Grandma Charlotte, Yolanda Williams, Kesha Lajoy Williams, Davie William, Vanessa William, Yogi William, Arleta, Tasha, the twins Nadine and Natalee, Marquell, Andre, Sherise Washington, Steven Shempert, Anna Mae, Irvin, Alicia, Jasmine, Marquita, Steve, Eric, Tony, Johnny Mae Palmer, LeeLee, Louis, my beloved Betty Walton, Nicholas, Divac, Vicki Sheldon, Natali Sheldon, Don, Pretty, Preacher, Gerald, Maryan, Kimberly Paige, Nicole Pitman, Nicole Sutton, Nakia Walton, Big O, Jasmine Randolph, and all others whom I love and has not mentioned here, stay strong! And thanks for loving me!

I cannot forget about those who have passed away during my captivity—Cabbage Patch, Chris,

Grandma Pinky, Lil Charles, Uncle Carl, Lil Jackie, Willie Hunt, Vendetta, my stepmother Rhonda Black, Aunt Ophelia, Georgia, Butch, Grandma Geraldine, Larry Harding, my mentor and brother for life, Denise Greenwood, Freeda, Uncle Donnell, cousin Sean, Aunt Fanny, Grandma Long, Gisselle, Poochie, Ronnie Rat, Leroy Ferguson, my beloved Great Aunt Marie Wilson (Aunt Bady), Dicky, Devan, Mike Watson, Mrs. Giggers, and my homeboy Mikey Wickliffe, RIP, my people! Until we meet again, you all will never be forgotten.

RIP to my baby brother Josh, my Aunty Maxine, my grandma Lucille, my Granddad Willie. My boys: Angelo, Kevin, and Yummy, and to everyone else who preceded me in death. You all live on in my heart!

Last but not least, to my nephews and nieces—AJ, Tee-tee, Maxine, Lil Larry, Larissa, Kee-Kee, Ireon, Cheezy Meezy, Kee-Kee #2, and the rest of the newly acquired cast that I haven't met yet. I love you all! Our time is coming soon. Thank y'all for loving me!

Finally, to Joshua Richard Sharp and Richard Sharp III, my beloved sons whom I love more than anything in the world. Thank you, guys, for being patient with me, and for waiting on me all of these years! I know I can't make up for all of the time that I missed out of your lives, but I can make our future together way better than our past was. You are my princes, my heart, and my joy! I am so proud of you guys! This book is for you guys, too. For along with your Grandma Elaine, you guys inspired me and gave me the hope to want to change and to do the right thing. Thank you my, princes! I love you both dearly!

Additional acknowledgements from Elaine Sharp:

Dr. Goosby & Staff of G.M. Pullman School, Dr. Maxine Toliver, Ms. Minnie Peggs & Staff of Miles Davis Academy, Dr. Kimberly Mann of Chicago State University (Social Work Dept.), Dr. J.A. Jones (Rehoboth C.O.G.I.C.), Pastor Fluker (Inspirations Church), Bishop Jones & Women & Men Group (South Side Tabernacle), Rev. and Co-Pastor House (New Life Baptist), Pastor Gregory Caffey (True Word Of Lift), Pastor Tina Arrington (Life Redeeming Ministries), My big brother Willie O. Smith and his wife Lisa Smith.

Special Friends: Maryann Miles-Browner, Joyce Thomas, Mr. Eddie Floyd, Steve Trice aka Stonewall, Pernetha Jeter, Salivie, Alvira & Fred McCaster, Bobby & Michael Harvey and Haitham & Zeyad (Roseridge Foods).

Dedicated to WORD-FIRST NFP, DASP and All Shades United, Organizations for change.

Introduction

It's been too long now that we have sat back and done nothing while the children of America's first original sin have been the victims of: racism, oppression, prejudice, fratricide, capitalism, and a host of other inhumane treatments which all work to bring a people down, even to the point of decimation.

Violence in the African-American (Black) community has reached deadly and almost extinctive proportions, especially when considering all of the young black males who are being incarcerated and warehoused like cattle for these offenses disproportionately. Yet all we hear from the people in power is: "lock them all up and give them more time" or "something has to be done about all of the violence that is going on in the African-American communities in this nation." It's been the same story for almost 100 years now, and not only have nothing changed, but in all actuality, things have gotten worse. So now I ask you, the reader of this book, *what is wrong with this picture?* Are we, as a nation, helpless in this matter? Or is it still like it's been since the inception of this problem: *people just don't care?*

In this book, *Black, White, and the Beginning of the End of Racism in America*, I will break down the roots of the problem from both sides of the spectrum. I will then work up through time from the start of the problem all the way up to our current date and time, and reveal truths and hidden feelings and ideologies from both sides which work to create these *racist mentalities* all across the spectrum, even with Latinos.

In discussing the *Beginning of the End of Racism in America*, I will display and magnify observable changes and growths in race relations in this country, and all of the things that all of us citizens of this country can do to finally eradicate this race problem and finally become one people and one nation with one solid vision for the future that will not only exalt our nation above all other nations, which have come before America and that will come after America, but will also, in the process, create a new *American*—the kind of American that the forefathers of this nation envisioned when they all got together and physically manifested their ideas, visions, and ideologies on this blessed soil in this western hemisphere. The solutions to our nation's race problem are simple, practical, and are easily implemental into the many institutions that govern our nation, society, and ways of life in all facets. I've come to realize that there are people on all sides that are so bitter and hateful that they have become incorrigible and are major *progress inhibitors* in our struggle for peace, love, and equality for all. I have also devised ways to work around these *hate-mongers* to prevent them from doing what they have been doing all history long, namely: being the problem en masse, sustaining long ran generational systems of hate, and continuously creating new confabulations to reinforce age-long and simplistically fallible racist ideologies that are the main culprits of poisoning the minds of the people, and thus creating and sustaining a new generation of racists.

Black, White, and the Beginning of the End of Racism in America is a blunt, heart-stopping, truth-filled book that is written to not only *start* the *conversation* about racism and the state of race relations here in America, but also to lay out a very simple and comprehensible step-by-step plan that will pragmatically change the way that Blacks and Whites perceive each other and engage one another in everyday life here in America.

The Beginning of the End of Racism in America is "all of us coming together regardless of color, race, nationality, ethnicity, ideology, creed, et cetera, and acknowledging our hidden predispositions toward others who are not what we consider to be *like us*!" This is the most important step that we can take in this modern age of *quarrel* where denial reigns supreme and ignorance is embraced as a cloak of protection. Once we learn to *keep it real* with ourselves and we begin to draw out all of the predispositional notions that are perpetually feeding our biases and we destroy them; all of the other steps and processes of ridding ourselves, our society of racism will automatically fall in line with little to no effort.

You have already taken the first step in ending racism in America by deciding to read this book. Congratulations! I encourage you to subdue, if not altogether destroy, any biases that you may have before reading this book so that you can be fully open and unbiased while digesting the truths written in this book in order for them to have the most optimal impact on your life and the dissolution of any remnant of witting or unwitting racism that may be hidden in your heart.

The ball is now in your court. I pray that you will embrace the truth that is written in this book, and allow for it to change you because we need you to change so you can change the world for us. I bid you good reading and peace! Our future as a nation depends on it!

Black: A Brief History

What does Adam, Eve, and all Homo sapiens have in common? They are all from the same source (GOD), from the same continent (Africa), and all share ninety-nine percent of the same DNA, with the one percent remaining being the celestial blueprint of GOD's divine spirit which also resides in all of us, and for man is the animating factor which gives the kinetic life force to all of man's biological and spiritual functions. Thus, every single person in the entire world share a common ancestor and creator, and are undoubtedly all related.

Now one may ask, "If this is all true and we are all related, then why do we all look different, act different, and have different cultures?" The most simple and comprehensive answer to this would be to say that "because our GOD loves diversity." This is very true! But understanding the way that GOD chooses to express diversity through *evolution* is the key to solving many myths, problems, and ignorantly devised mundane doctrines and indoctrinations that continue to widen the gaps of separation that exist between the so-called races, nationalities, and ethnic groups of our species. In this work, I will break down this divine process in the simplest manner as if to make the understanding behind this glorious divine process so easy to comprehend that even a child could grasp and understand its meaning. Thus, properly understood, this knowledge and under-standing of GOD's divine process of evolution will change the way that mankind sees each other and treat each other, for God made all of us *perfect* in all of our diversity.

Race is an *illusion*; it doesn't exist! It was created by man in an attempt for *some* to rule over all the *rest*. For it is always the minority, wherever they may be found or whatever they may be doing, to come up with such divisive tools and concepts in order to maintain control and some sort of power over every-one else that isn't a part of their group. And to prove that racism is an illusion, let us consider these facts: (1) both theological and scientific Adam and Eve came from Africa at a time when the only people in the world were dark skinned people (so-called *black* people); (2) we all share the same DNA as theologi-cal and scientific Adam and Eve, thus making us all related in some form or another; and (3) all outer variations of the human race are due to environment adaptations and are genetically suitable for each cli-mate pertaining to the peoples that are inhabiting those environments. So basically, to hate another human being because of their group affiliations or the color or texture of their hair or skin is likened unto hating one of your two children who were both conceived by the same parents because one has red hair and full lips, unlike the brown hair and thin lips that the rest of the family has.

This sounds ridiculous, doesn't it? Well, when one is biased (so-called racist) toward the other variations of our species, he or she is actually partaking in the same folly as mentioned above. We are all the same, my human brothers and sisters! The small external variations that we share, each in accordance with their *geographical group* (tribe) were designed to appropriately adapt us and acclimatize us to our respective environments so that each group could not only survive but also flourish in such environments without being at the complete mercy of the elements (nature).

People from warmer regions have: color, wider noses, less body hair, and more times than not, what's known as the *steatopygia* gene.

People from colder regions have: little to no color, thinner and longer noses, more body hair, straighter hair, and more times than not, an assortment of lighter colored eyes.

Each individual or group are perfectly suited for their environment. Things are so perfect that it would be hard to try to fathom such a perfectly orchestrated and complex biological system without the idea of *intelligent design*. Thus, just because externally one may be a little bit different, that doesn't, by any means, make him or her deficient. Given each individual or group placed in their evolutionary environment (indigenous continent of evolutionary development/mutation after leaving Africa) will have some advantages that their other relatives of the species may not have in that particular environment, the same advantages apply to that other group in their evolutionary environment as well.

We, as humans, need to start truthfully educating ourselves and especially our young with the truth about why we look the way we look, and how being biased toward others who doesn't look the way we look is not only ignorance in its rawest form but is also a blight against our creator in the form of saying that what he, the most perfect *architect* of all, designed and created isn't *good*! If this is what God made and called *good* on the sixth day, then who are you to say it's not? We, as a species, need to check ourselves and progress past the stages of ignorance and bigotry, and begin to function as *cohesive human beings* before we destroy one another and all cease to exist as a species.

GOD knew what he was doing when he moved us out of Africa and led us all over this planet. As the environments began to change in the different regions of the world, so did the life forms that inhabited those environments. Those that didn't adapt quick enough were soon became extinct. And all those that did, lived on and preserved their genes with all of their new mutations for their progeny.

The first group of Africans that inhabited what is now known as the continent of Europe were the first Europeans, and no, *they weren't white*. They were people of color; the so-called *black* people. They are the progenitors of every single white person that has ever lived, for with them was the mutation born which caused a recession in: pigmentation, thickness of hair, and cranial structure development in order to accommodate the new physiognomy that would be needed in order to adapt to the new hostile environment that they were inhabiting.

Depigmented skin was necessary to maximize the small amount of sunlight that fell upon the peoples' bodies, especially during the last ice age when the *New* European people were cut off from the rest of the world via glaciers and ice sheets, and most of the sun's rays were reflected back from outer space by the snow and ice. Thus, pigmentation was not optimal for such an environment.

Thinner noses were necessary to not only prevent from breathing in too much cold air, which in return could crystalize the lungs and also cause numerous other malignant maladies, but also to make way for longer nasal cavities and membranes to warm up the cold air more effectively before it enters the lungs.

Hair texture, as mentioned above, also evolved as an adaptation to climate. Straight hair grows faster than wooly hair, and is also made up of more strands than woolly hair. Hair is needed in such cold environbents in order to insulate the body and help to hold on to heat which is so vital for body maintenance and functioning in such a hostile climate.

It's the opposite with people of African descent who descends down from those original inhabitants that remained behind and continued their evolution on the very warm and mostly humid African continent. They maintained their pigment because it was needed to protect the skin and organs beneath it from excessive exposure to ultraviolet radiation from the sun.

They maintained less body hair so as to allow for sweat to evaporate quicker, thus keeping the body cooler. And their wider (platyrrhine) noses with shorter nasal passages and membranes cooled and balanced the air for the lungs instead of heating it up. Thick woolly hair, especially on the top of the head, protected the brain under conditions of extreme heat. Everything about every single person in the world is *perfect* and *beautiful*. We are all from the same mother and father; the first of our kind who produced all of us. So remember, just because you have white skin with blue eyes and your wife has white skin with blues eyes, doesn't mean that you're son with the brown skin and brown eyes isn't your son. *Atavism* (throwback genes) happens to all gene pools from time to time.

We are all variations of the same *prototype* (Adam), so how can one be a racist when racism doesn't really exist? Only through sheer ignorance can one hate that which he or she doesn't understand. And with the race standards and race codes that humanity has created to help to regulate peoples and the world en masse, it appears only as an illusionary vision that racism can be completely ended in America, let alone in the world.

Before we can even think about the world, though, we must fix our own problems here at home first. That starts with the great rift that separates so-called whites from the descendants of the slaves that they brought here to this country many centuries ago in chains: the *Africans,* or nowadays called *African-Americans.* The African-Americans' history is a unique one. To fully understand how (did we get to this point) and why African-Americans have the perspectives that they have about the world in general and about white people, let us first understand: *what is an African-American?*

The Making of the African-American

Unlike every other so-called: race, nationality, and ethnicity (with the exception of Native Americans) that have come to America of their own volition. African-Americans are the only group of people that were brought to this country forcibly in chains and weren't even deemed as being humans but only property for to be both, sold, traded and used in whatever fashion their owners (masters) seen fit to use them in. This unique history alone is enough to shape and influence the perspectives of these descendants of African slaves (African-Americans), not to mention the leaving behind of generations and generations' worth of psychological trauma which also works to mold the perspectives of these people and create *predispositions* toward whites and American society as a whole.

In order for you to be able to understand the *African-American* and why they are the way they are, you must first know and understand *what an African-American is*.

Most so-called *Blacks* in America don't even consider themselves as African-American, especially among the males of the group. To be called an African-American is even considered to be an insult by some African-Americans, or shall I say, *people of African descent.* So what is an *African - American*, and why is their *ethos* the way it is? For those of you who don't know already, I encourage you to take a deep breath and open up your minds in order for you to prepare yourself to receive this unconventional truth that will not only change your perspective on how you see African-Americans but will also help you to really understand why the social, economic, political, and psychological conditions that the African-American finds his and herself in today's times in these United States of America are so destructive for them. Please pay close attention and keep an open, unbiased mind, my white, brown, yellow, and all non-African-American brothers and sisters, and allow for the truth to increase your understanding so that you, too, can play your part in helping to do away with racism in this beautiful country that we all must inhabit together.

The descendants of African slaves who are now identified as *African-Americans* have a unique history and strange beginnings as an ethnic group here in America.

The first Africans to come to America were in chains, and were victims of kidnappings and property exchanges between whites and blacks/Arabs of different ethnic backgrounds and from different parts of the African continent.

Once the Africans arrived in America and were sold off at slave markets like property, the first thing that their white slave masters did to them was for his or her slave breakers to break the African's will to be human and his or her will to resist his or her new identity as only property whose sole purpose was only to obey and fulfill their masters' every command or desire.

This was done to the Africans by taking away their identities that defined who they were before they were kidnapped and taken away as slaves, forbidding them to speak their natural tongues which communicated their history, culture, family traditions, etc., and by giving them all new identities which were only beneficial in emphasizing their inferiority, dependency upon keeping the master happy so that they could survive here in America, and inculcating in them a kind of psychological programing that would be systematically passed down from generation to generation by the slaves themselves automatically, thus sustaining perpetually the institution of slavery and the inferiority complex of blacks knowing their place in America as the land that was made by white men for white men but was built mostly by the so-called black man. So the making of the African-American was a methodically carried out plan that involved no sense of humanity whatsoever.

After being kidnapped, stripped naked, beaten, placed on a boat and packed up like sardines in a can for a month, brought to shore and sold like a box of candy that has no real life value, humiliated, dehumanized, and last but not least, taught to see the world in complete anomie outside of serving their masters, what was left of these once glorious and supremely spiritual people was no more than a body that was all but *undead*. The only thing that the Africans had going for them is the very same thing that worked to sustain them and to hold on to as much as their former ways of being as possible, and that was their innate sense of GOD (spirituality), with their supreme beliefs that "GOD was in control of everything" and that "everything that existed was a manifestation of GOD in some form or manner."

Despite their new identities that were being forced on them along with all of its traditions, customs, and so-called *plantation morals*, the African slaves managed to maintain their spirituality in part, whether it was Juju, Islam, Hebrewism, or any of their various forms of animism by incorporating the traditions and concepts of these spiritual forms of expression into their slave form of Christianity by which their masters permitted them to practice on their plantations.

Over the next 250 years, these Africans in America were bred like animals, sold all over the country, and traded off as payments for debts, favors, or just all in jest. The psychological and the biological damage that resulted from the 250 years of brutal inhumane treatment left the Africans in America discombobulated, inept for society, disenfranchised, and doomed to roam around the soil of America in complete anomie without no sense of being, identity, sustenance, or humanity toward one another, seeing that they were treated as and inculcated into seeing themselves as property rather than human beings.

This is the history of the so-called *African-American*. This was their lot until their so-called *emancipation* in 1865. After 1865, they were all just thrust into society without any *pre-assimilation* systems set up in order to help them learn the culture, educate themselves in the idiosyncrasies of that culture, or to equip them in order to be able to properly compete in an extremely sophisticated and harum-scarum capitalistic culture such as the U.S economic culture.

Now, add on to this miserable and unfortunate condition of the African-Americans all the opposing forces that would come up in order to inhibit the progress of their assimilation into the American culture from 1865 until even today, such as the Klan, Black Codes (Jim Crow), institutional racists (i.e., lawmakers, clergymen, judges, school teachers, etc.), and a biased organic system which was designed to suppress the only three-fifths of a man *a.k.a.* black man from ever rising up from the status of mere property into a *human being*. Then, you get this creature of circumstance which America and her social order has created, and is now forced to have to deal with. Yes! America is now *reaping* the results of the seeds that she has sown in the act of committing her *original sin* of kidnapping/slavery.

The African-American has been shaped by circumstances unlike anything that has been seen by modern man. We are a peculiar people with a history and beginnings unlike no other group on this planet. Unlike other groups in this country which freely migrated to this nation of their own volition, the African-American was betrayed, kidnapped, and even sold into slavery, and brought into this nation involuntarily in chains and in shackles in the nude.

Also, unlike other races and groups in this country, the African-American does not have an accepted culture of their own outside of America to fall back on. Yes, the African-American does not have this fortification for authentic identity and self-respect.

The impulsiveness, aggression, improvidence, selfishness, immorality, etc., that are manifested by most African-Americans in this nation aren't the results of just slavery alone, but are also significantly motivated by the lack of knowledge of who they were during pre-slave trade.

We, as a whole, are not a destructive people who are bent on blaming the white man for all of our problems and our overall condition in America. Howsoever, we, as a people, also do not completely absolve the white man/system from the part he played and the part that's systematically still being played in creating and maintaining the main destructive elements that are working to destroy the African-American people in this country.

The African-American is a spiritual being taking up residence in a physical body for a short time;

a resilient being that refuses to give up despite the astronomical odds that aren't ever in his favor in just about anything that he does here in this land of his captivity. He, like everyone else in this land, seeks only to love and be loved, live a healthy, peaceful, and prosperous life, and last but not least, try to achieve and live the *American dream* with as little problems as possible.

This is the *African-American*.

Christianity as the Foundation of African-American Culture

Christianity has played a major role in the formation of the African-American's psyche and culture. Though the form of Christianity that was originally received by the then African slaves was only a mere projection of true Christianity or even the version of Christianity that was being practiced by white society at the time, it had both authentic and inauthentic parts of Christianity which were then amalgamated with indigenous African traditions and customs, which had survived the slave trade and indoctrinations of the slave masters, and were being preserved through griots and diverse African scholars who were now slaves here in America without their new American slave masters having the slightest clue of the intelligence, skill, and culture that they possessed. A new Christianity, a kind of Afrocentric Christianity, was now being born which was peculiar to the African slaves and encompassing all of their struggles, plights, longings, and spiritually utopic climaxes.

This new black form of Christianity would later be known as *Black Liberation Theology*, and outside of placing all of one's faith in Jesus Christ, this theology also taught the liberation of the black people from the oppressive pangs of the white slave master and his entire slave culture/civilization. The self-development and uplifting of all Black people by their own means with the help of Jesus Christ, the great liberator himself, and the perceiving of all things from a Black perspective instead of the inculcated perspective of the whitewashed slave mentality which was and still is even until this day the *dominant mentality* of the vast majority of African-Americans.

From generation to generation, from slavery until now, this black form of Christianity would be embraced, extolled, culturally drilled into the innermost being of the Africans in America, and practically applied to every aspect of the African-Americans' culture, life, and holistic being in their new home here in America.

At the turn of the nineteenth century, almost all African-Americans were some denomination of Christian, or either had some type of faith in Jesus Christ. In the twentieth century, with the advent of Islam in America, a nice percentage of blacks began to cross over and convert to Islam, which most of the blacks began to perceive as the *black man's religion*, the great truth that would deliver them form the white man's religion of *Christianity*, and the White man's civilization, *America.*

Though both religions were embraced by blacks, these two religions presented blacks with two separate ethos, which in time, would further divide black people, and in a sense, do more harm than good.

On the one hand, you had Christianity teaching the blacks to be humble, submit to their slave masters and to people in authority, to turn the other cheek, to forgive indiscriminately regardless of the gravity of the offense or the debauchery, and to love your enemy unconditionally.

On the other hand, you had Islam teaching love, unity, solidarity of means, and supreme justice. However, there were also denominations of Islam that many of the blacks accepted that taught the white man as a *blue-eyed devil*, America is the *great whore of Babylon*, and that separation of the races is better than integration.

These African-Americans viewed the Christian African-Americans (or at least, the *nonviolent* ones) as Uncle Toms and betrayers of the black race.

These perceptions have persisted even until this day, and still works to help divide the African-American community and inhibit their quest for universal unity which has never successfully happened ever since they've been in America.

With the vast majority of African-Americans identifying themselves as Christians or just plain *believers in Christ*, the Islamic proportion of African-Americans are far inferior in numbers in comparison to their Christian counterparts. Nonetheless, there are still enough of them in number to continue to maintain the riff that exists between African-American Christians and African-American Muslims here in America.

The Christian cadre of the African-American community is so strong that its influence howsoever still has the force to infiltrate and regulate to a certain degree the mental and behavioral patterns of African-American Muslims regardless of their devotion to Islam. Most of these Muslims came from Christian families, thus the values and morals of Christianity were instilled inside of them ever since they were born and has become an indelible part of their overall development and being.

The holy Bible as a problem-solving nexus for African-Americans is a given. It's much a part of African-American culture as their thought forming process and finality of decisions that every single African-American in America, at some point in time, has been influenced by the Bible. The church still is the staple of the African-American community even though its strength, influence, and authority have waned over the years. However, the fact still remains as was spoken by Margaret Sanger, saying, "The most successful educational approach to the negro is through religious appeal." Black people, as a whole, tend to be predisposed to spirituality. Even the lowest of the race has a quality of spirituality that regulates their natural decision-making processes.

Now, one can see how whether it is Islam, Christianity, Judaism, Buddhism, Animism, etc. that comes across the path of the African, or anyone of African descent, the quickness of acceptance and attentiveness that is displayed by them in appropriating the diverse religious doctrines and tenets into their everyday lives.

There is an innate receptor which exists inside of black people which causes even the most depraved of the race to halt or pause at the sound of *spirituality*. Religion/spirituality is extremely *attention getting* for blacks. Thus, even though Christianity was forced upon the first African-Americans that were brought to this country as slaves and it was modified and evolved by them to that of a more familiar Afrocentric form of spirituality, the impact of the religion still was strong enough to influence and become the foundation of African-American culture and stand the test of time, for even until this day, Christianity remains the dominant vanguard of the African-American race and the standard value system of the African-American community.

The Effect of Slavery
and Segregation on the
African-Americans' Psyche

The impact of slavery and segregation upon the lives and psyches of the African-American people is an indelible and purpose changing one.

Biologically, the damage that has been done from hundreds of years of eating foods that are unfit for human consumption (i.e., pork [chitterlings, pig feet, pig ears], grits, collard greens, catfish, crabs, sugar water, etc.) is only one side of the coin. The gravest damage of all was done to the African-American psychologically.

The evil use of white and white American theories on African-Americans has been destructive upon them ever since they were first exacted upon them on the North American continent. You can't take an entire people who weren't even considered people but was considered only *three-fifths of a man* who were held in a system of chattel slavery for 245 years, and just released them into a capitalistic society without any pre-assimilation systems setup in order to help them learn the culture, educate themselves in the idiosyncrasies of that culture, and last but not least, prepare them to be able to *equally* compete in this competitive capitalistic society where only the strongest succeeds while the weakest gets trampled upon and categorized as the lowest caste only to be shunned, stigmatized, programed, and kept out of the thriving sector of society as pariahs and liabilities. This is the *cause* of the modern *effect* of Black culture, mentation, self-deprecation, and the violence that plagues our inner cities, prisons, and mostly every other location where blacks (specifically *African-Americans*) are found to be in high numbers.

Reconstruction was the government's move to accommodate all of the assimilation processes mentioned above for its newly freed slaves, and thus try to prevent this modern condition of African-Americans by which they are suffering through right now. It is a known fact that reconstruction, as it was designed to be in its true progressive form, really died with the death of President Abraham Lincoln. Not only did the freed slaves (African-Americans) not receive the proverbial *forty acres and a mule* that was promised to them by congress via the *Freedmen's Bureau*, but to add insult to injury, the land that had been confiscated from the insurrectionary states by the Federal government that was to be used to allocated the forty-acre quota to the freed slaves was astonishingly rerouted back to the enslavers in fear of white landowners in the South becoming disenfranchised. This left the newly emancipated slaves with *nothing*.

They had no land, no money, no assets, no education, nothing! They were tossed into a capitalistic society with all of these 250 years' worth of disadvantages, and were placed against a group of people—the dominant group of people, I may add—who had benefited and capitalized on the 250 years of the slaves' disadvantages and who, by no means necessary, was ever going to level the playing field for their lifelong inferiors to ever have any chance to compete, let alone thrive, in the capitalistic system of America. Thus, just like in slavery and now even after slavery, the African-Americans were doomed from the start.

Most of the slaves, if not all, were already psychologically scarred before they were even emancipated. Any functioning human being knows that the mind is the seat of the real battle with any person, and if you control someone's mind and the way that they think, then you can control their whole body, and also their destiny for that matter.

This psychological scarring of the minds of the slaves was a deliberate action that was methodically carried out for many generations by the slave masters, and also those whites who had the predisposed inclinations to believe that *all Blacks are naturally inferior to all whites.* One of the most widespread methods that were used to psychologically break the slave's mind and will was called the *Willie Lynch Method.* Willie Lynch, a vicious and inhuman slave owner/slave breaker from Barbados Island, knew that if he could find a way to control the psyches of the slaves that he could program them into carrying out his brainwashing propaganda forever from generation to generation without anyone ever having to stand on them to make them do so. This was the greatest desire of all slave masters and prejudiced whites together—to have all Black people to be programmed in an automatizing manner that would ensure the slave master that the slaves would never rebel against them, plot against them and their interests, kill or exact retribution against them or their progeny for the horrors and consequences of slavery, and no matter what, always remember their places as inferiors in America and to the white man to whom he must always depend upon for sustenance, guidance, civilization, and protection against himself as well as from all others who despise him.

Willie Lynch inculcated into the slaves' minds dependency upon the slave master and white people, the fear of white people, envy of white people and their culture, and self-perpetuating enmity between light skinned blacks and dark skinned blacks, also between the black man and black woman. All of these destructive tendencies were indoctrinated, inculcated, and literally beaten into the minds of black people for hundreds of years nonstop. Is there any reason why the African-American is so messed up now?

America and the black man's unique history in America bears most of the responsibility for the conditions that African-American now find themselves in. This can no longer be denied or ignored if we, as a nation, are to finally heal the wounds of the past, and begin to actually move into *tomorrow's world* together as one united nation indivisible with liberty and justice for all!

Most African-Americans don't hate white people. It just appears that way sometimes because, believe it or not, most African-Americans don't understand white people. The reason they don't understand them is because most of them didn't grow up around any white people. They have only encountered them in places like events, prisons, courthouses, hospitals, etc. These encounters are not enough to get to know someone or their group's ethos, thus there is a great divide that separates blacks and whites, especially the blacks from urban areas which constitutes approximately ninety-two percent of the African-American population here in the U.S.

Post Traumatic Slave Syndrome or PTSS is a real and observable disease which affects just about every single African-American alive today, especially those living in the United States.

PTSS, as is reflected in its title, is a direct result of slavery. Once you add the many other atrocities which befell the blacks in America after they were freed from slavery like: Black Codes, lynchings, disenfranchisement, and all of the biases of segregation into the equation, you come out with a psychologically damaged and diseased people. Even in today's time, PTSS is still being reinforced through racism, institutional racism, social policies, inequality, oppression, and through many forms of covert white supremacy. Segregation is still a reality. Anyone who doesn't believe this only has to look as far as the church, the school system, the criminal justice system, the economic system, and society as a whole, whereas in every state and every town or city, you have your areas which are predominantly black, white, or Hispanic. Even this voluntary selective settlement of the races reflects the attitudes and pathos of racism, albeit in a more incognito manner. This, too, reinforces the African-American's PTSS. For even when he puts in the appropriate work and discipline to finally be able to move out of his dilapidated community and attempts to move into a community of higher value, which are more times than not going to be a community which is predominantly white, he is opposed by forces from all sides which will not relent at keeping him out of these white esteemed upper-class communities. Thus, his situation and his perspective on life in America as an American, let alone an African-American, is one of chronic hopelessness and self-deprecating skepticism. These views and feelings are the seeds of the destructive tendencies and ethos of the African-American.

The African-Americans have been psychologically attacked from the start. Until all that has been done to the African-Americans is undone, the misery and destruction of these people will continue to worsen, and America, as a whole, will have to deal with the consequences of the African-American's depraved condition

How Did We Get Here?

We are at a crucible in race relations here in the U.S, with our murky past leading the way and still influencing events, idiosyncrasies, and individual thought patterns. We are at a point in time where we, as a nation, will rise or fall due to the relationships between the races and their ability to respect one another and work together for the common good.

Years and years of hate, racism, segregation, and Willie Lynch directed toward the black race by the white race here in America have brought us to this present moment of time wherein chaos and confusion reign supreme. As stated earlier, the slaves, even after slavery ended, were forced to deal with a country where the people hated them, and the laws of the land which regulated the behavior of the citizens of the land were written for their former masters and their master's kin in order to maintain the perpetual status quo of white supremacy (white privilege) and not for the blacks by which many still believed to not only be inferior to whites but also to only be three-fifths of a human being.

Then, out of slavery and wandering around aimlessly in a nation where they were the *persona non grata* at every turn, they still had to try to conceptualize slavery's new form known as *Jim Crow*. Jim Crow further held back their progress and inhibited their assimilation into society. Although Jim Crow (named after an early black minstrel song) was mainly a system of segregation and discrimination against blacks in America, many blacks were lynched and murdered in its name.

Brown vs. the Board of Education in 1954, was supposed to end segregation once and for all in America. Doing away with the previous ruling/standard, Plessy vs Ferguson (1896) which was ruled on by the U.S Supreme Court stated that the *separate but equal doctrine* was constitutional.

Although the Supreme court ruling on Brown vs. Board of Education of Topeka, Kansas (1954) struck down the *separate but equal doctrine* as unconstitutional, most people don't realize that the Brown vs. Board of Education ruling focused more on separation than equality, and the separation aspect of the problem was only one-fourth of the problem. The more significant part of the problem which is the issue of *racial, social, and economic equality* was all but ignored and still is even unto this day. If it were not so, then there would be no need for this book.

The damage of slavery, racism, Willie Lynch, and capitalism has been so deeply and generationally internalized inside of the minds of African-Americans to the point where their development as human beings in America and as so-called American citizens will forever be different and unique in itself, no other human being in America had its origins in the horrific forms of the origins of the so-called African-American.

With the exception of the Native American and the African-American, everyone else in this country is an immigrant, which means that they optionally by choice decided to come here. The African-American had no such choice but were brought here in chains, stripped of their history and culture, and forced to endure for 245 years some of the most inhumane atrocities which could ever be conceived of.

The African-American's history, status, and perspective in this nation is a unique one that could really only be understood by the African-Americans themselves, for only they had to endure it and survive it.

The so-called uncultured, unmannered, ignorant, super aggressive, and destructive African-American that is seen today in America is the result of what the European (white) American sowed almost 400 years ago. We are reaping now the results of what was sown then.

The founding fathers of this nation knew that this would happen one day, and in an attempt to try to control it if not altogether prevent it, they legislated the 13th Amendment which says, "Neither slavery nor involuntary servitude, except as a punishment for crime whereof the party shall have been duly convicted, shall exist within the United States, or any place subject to their jurisdiction." so To maintain control over blacks and subtly reinstitute slavery, the *penal institution* (prison) would become the new plantation.

Prison is a big business now that everyone has their hands in, and to make sure that they stay full, the powers that be have designed several crafty machinations to assure the wardens that the body count will always be on point.

Over legislation and draconian laws have decimated the black male population here in the U.S It's bad enough that blacks has a higher probability than anyone else in America to end up in jail, prison, or on some type of government supervision, but to legislate harsher punishment, which are specifically directed at minorities, is a direct racial statement that displays a hidden agenda which is being obscured by those in power, and also a lack of empathy for all minorities regardless of their backgrounds or their predispositions toward crime due to their environments and lack of opportunities to move up in the world.

The negation of choices from people of color in correlation to their white counterparts is another strong reason why things are the way that they are here in twenty-first century America. For example, if you have two fools (one black and one white) with equal intelligence, and you give them both choices to choose their paths of life and the opportunities which comes with it, only you give the black three choices and the white ten choices, logic dictates that the similarly foolish white will have an extremely higher probability of being successful than his equally foolish black counterpart, only because he has more opportunities which are more chances to get it right in the event that he fails one of the other nine times.

This has been happening ever since the white man has encountered the black man anywhere and everywhere, even on the African's own continent. To be born black anywhere where the white culture is the dominant culture is always a born disadvantage. History has proven this fact time and time again. For to be born black in a white man's society and in poverty with little or no resources has disaster written all over it.

Poverty and frustration are great catalysts for violence. These are the key components that are mainly responsible for the violence and crime that we are continuing to see in African-American communities all over America. The legacy of slavery cannot be overlooked or ignored any longer if there is to be any real reconciliation between the races. America has failed the oppressed descendants of her original sin! Social, economic, and all culturally assimilating attempts to uplift and to empower the descendants of African slaves in this country have failed. The results of these failures have led to the modern conditions of the African-American and their plights. Now, it has all but been proven by the actions of the U.S government that the deprived and wanton condition of blacks in America is of no importance to them, though members of all races and ethnicities are nowadays a part of the government here in America. The decisions that are made at the top, which then trickles down to the bottom and affects the masses which are always at the bottom of the social ladder anywhere wherever they are encountered, are made by not just white people anymore. All peoples participate in these decisions in today's America, yet from the perspective of the blacks, it still all falls down on the white man. Any decision that is made or any rule or law that is made which has any form of impact on the lives of African-Americans will be perceived by them to have been decided by and handed down by *the white man*. History, or shall I say the *peculiar* history that all African-Americans share in common, has placed inside of their hearts this amoral disposition toward whites (especially the ones in power) which applies to all avenues by which the two races ever has to deal with one another or come into any realm of influence upon one another in America or anywhere else in the world. Thus, the predominate black thought about white people is one of the unique substance with an extraordinary history behind it.

To learn why even today in the twenty-first century America we still have the same racist attitudes toward one another, we will dive into the predominant black thought about whites and America in the next chapter of this book. Later on, we will also dive into the predominant white thought about black people and America, too.

Until we can understand why these *predominant thoughts* still reside within the minds of these peoples of various and diverse races toward each other, we cannot possibly conceive of coming up with, let alone implement, a program or means by which to eliminate such thoughts from the minds of such people, and thus begin to usher in a time of universal, racially acceptable peace, unity, and love with one another.

It all starts where it will all end—*in the minds of the people.* Let us now grasp these thoughts and take every thought captive which is not conducive to the greater good of our cause. For it is now or never for us as a country and a people. Either we are all going to be one as Americans, or it will continue to be every race, nationality, and ethic group for themselves, as we all compete for a larger piece of the *American pie.* The thoughts about each other by each other will determine the fate of the nation soon enough. So what are these *predominate thoughts* that I speak of? Let's enter the mind of the African-American first, then we will work toward the predominant white thought about blacks and America.

The Predominant Black Thought about White People and America

I understand that I cannot and do not speak for all black people. So to all of my black and very beautiful brothers and sisters who are found all throughout America, I only speak what has been found by me to be the *truth*. In dealing with self and with you, I have come to discover that which most of us try to conceal in diverse attempts to not seem racist. It's become a norm for blacks to act one way around blacks, and another way around whites. Just as the Declaration of Independence and the Constitution are of two different spirits which neither bears witness with the spirit of African-Americans, blacks in America have evolved to be of two different spirits here in America, especially when dealing with white people.

Very few blacks today, unlike blacks in the past, have the tendency to want to be white or *white-like*. And though most blacks won't admit it, there is a thought of blame that is directed toward white people for the conditions that we find ourselves in. It doesn't always translate into hate or violence, but more of a type of innate incredulity. The main reason why most blacks are unwilling to believe or trust whites all stems from the legacy of slavery in one form or another. This unbelief and skepticism toward whites are reasonably justified for the following reasons: (1) White Americans then nor now never accepted responsibility for the destruction done to the African-American race *via* slavery or the systematic inhibitors which succeeded slavery, and in most cases, done even more damage to African-Americans than slavery itself (i.e., Jim Crow, economic bias, mass incarceration of blacks, caste systems, etc.); (2) The failure of whites both then and now to even acknowledge slavery or try to even attempt to understand its impact and infinitude, like influence upon the African-Americans' entire being as a whole; and (3) Whites continue to ignore the fact that the reason that they have such a large economic advantage over African-Americans is because of the vast amounts of wealth that they accumulated during and from the free labors of black slaves in American from 1619 until 1865.

The African/African-American never received any type of compensation whatsoever after slavery ended. Thus, as stated earlier, "They were just thrust into society with no economic assets which were needed to, at minimum, be able to compete with whites in a very competitive capitalistic society." They found themselves in most situations worse off than they were while still on the plantations.

Most African-Americans in today's times believe that there can never be any real reconciliation between the black and white races without some form of *reparations* for the descendants of African slaves (themselves).

It is undeniable that the wealth gap, underdevelopment, and social/economic disadvantages that are shared by African-Americans are direct results of the 245 years of slavery that they had to endure, coupled with another 100 years of Jim Crow and societal ostracism which they faced at every turn of the corner no matter where they went. Thus, *reparations* are not only a good gesture toward African-Americans and the pursuit of reconciliation and the ending of racism between blacks and whites here in America, but are actually a prerequisite if the two races are to really be able to finally move on from the legacy of slavery and the unhealthy predominant thoughts that both groups subtly keep hidden from each other.

I understand that most whites tremble at the sound of the blacks receiving reparations for slavery, especially in monetary value. But I challenge those whites that think like that to consider this: reparations were paid to the following groups in these amounts by the United States of America: Alaska natives (1971)—$1 billion and 44 million acres of land; Klamath of Oregon (1980)—$81 million; Lakota of South Dakota (1985)—$105 million; and Japanese-Americans (1990) —$1.2 billion. There are other groups also that have received payments for reparations from the United States. I will not mention those groups at this moment, however, the fact remains that reparations were paid out to other groups. No disrespect to these other groups, but no one has suffered nor had to suffer like the Africans/African-Americans here in the U.S. Even the descendants of these slaves are still living through the legacy of slavery here in America even until this day, their total being of functioning is influenced *via* the legacy of slavery. Until this issue is addressed and dealt with accordingly, there will be no trust between the races, and if there is no trust between the races, there can *never* be any peace between the races. A lot of African-Americans think this way about whites and the system. The *system* in African-American culture is synonymous with *white power* and the white power structure. Blacks can't trust, either, and they believe that both long to see them destroyed if they can't find a way to return them back to their former state of slavery.

Now let me inform you that the mind-set of older blacks is completely different than that of younger blacks nowadays. This phenomenon can also be perceived on the opposite side of the spectrum among whites. But we will deal with the white aspect of things later. For now, though, we shall remain focused on the black side of things

Older blacks both male and female from let's say age forty on up distrust white people significantly higher than younger black males and females do. Younger blacks (both sexes), especially within the age group of thirteen to twenty-five years old tend to only not distrust white people, but in a lot of cases, tend to be rather fond of them. This reason is basically because American culture, as a whole, is more accepting now than ever of diverse groups and their particularisms. So a lot of African-American particularisms that were once viewed as abhorrent by white culture (the dominant culture), are now not only being accepted by white culture but are, more times than not, being ingrained into white culture nowadays. This is creating a new type of white American. Though younger and more tolerant than their older white counterparts, these new white Americans still are filled with what almost seems like an *innate* sense of privilege (white privilege) which comes out from time to time when they are faced with situations with other racial groups especially situations involving intelligence and race.

I believe that this innate sense of privilege is constantly being reinforced inside of whites by their domination of American culture. As early as their senses began to operate as children, they began to see, and in most cases, are even taught about their dominance in America and abroad. This is then reinforced with everything that they see and are taught from a Eurocentric perspective. Their dolls and toys are white, their language English is white, and their customs, values, and traditions are all white. Then, there is the *beauty standard* which is supremely white and is standardized by the value of all-European (white) features.

Now, can you see the type of impact that such propaganda can have on all others that are foreign to all of the ideals, concepts, and so-called standards of everything that I mentioned above?

This is significantly worse for blacks than anyone else, for the simple fact that not only were blacks slaves and property of whites in this country for all those hundreds of years, but that they were forced to assimilate into the society with these same people and their oppressive views which had worked to keep them subjugated and inferior for all of those years. This is why the social and cultural gaps between blacks and whites are so far apart, thus the predominant thoughts of both races concerning one another.

In closing this chapter, I would just like to add that while writing this book, five Dallas police officers were killed and several other police officers were wounded by gunfire from a twenty-five-year-old black male named Mica. Mica's motives for the shootings were that he said that he was tired of the police, especially white police, shooting and killing black men for no reason. Thus, he resolved to shoot and kill as many white policemen as possible before being killed himself.

Unbeknownst to white America is the fact that Mica's mind frame and course of action, which resulted from his mind frame, isn't an isolated or spontaneous incident. The vast majority of African-American males (especially those who grew up in the *hood*) who grew up here in America feels like Mica felt, and if they could kill police (especially white police) and get away with it, they would.

There is so much going on in the minds of black males that the whites have no idea about. This is because of the inability of whites to want to reach out to the African-American community, and to try to understand the ethos of blacks and why they think the way that they think and behave the way they behave.

Thus, changing, or so-called reforming, institutional systems in this country will not affect any type of change between the black and white races in this country for the simple fact that all of these systems/institutions are dominated by whites who mostly have little or no understanding about blacks, their culture, their ethos, and definitely no understanding about why they think the way they do. This lack of knowledge and understanding creates a kind of fear in these whites which tend to be carried out in the form of passive aggressive legislation and various modes of systemic and institutionalized racism. Over policing the black community is another expression of white ignorance and fear, and is also the cause of most of it, if not all, of the white on black killings that are constantly being carried out by white police officers on black males.

It is almost a severe tragedy to place young uninformed white males into black communities to police such communities with the lack of knowledge and understanding that is consistently displayed by these white officers when dealing with black people in inner city black neighborhoods. These encounters almost always end badly.

Black people are aware of the fanatical and inexorably hysterical behavior that white police officers display while policing their communities. It is a known fact that *aggression breeds aggression*, so when these white police officers behave in the said manner toward blacks, it exacerbates the situation and makes physical conflict inevitable.

In black thought, it goes that the police represent the enemy which is the *system*. The system represents all things anti-African-American (i.e., all of the main sources of livelihood) dating all the way back to the founding of the system itself by the founding fathers of these United States of America who didn't even consider Blacks/African-Americans as human beings but only as property to be disposed of and used in whatever way their owners saw fit.

America's most sacred document, the Constitution, reflects the abovementioned truths and works to confirm and perpetuate the progressive ideals, vision, and prophetic destiny which were prophesied by the founding fathers upon all future generations of white Americans and the modifications by which to view and deal with their black inhuman property.

Even in their Declaration of Independence which was written by Thomas Jefferson, who ironically was a slave holder/slave molester himself, had for his legislative assembly in Virginia pass his *A Bill* concerning slaves, restricting the movements of slaves, and requiring white women who bear mulatto children to leave the commonwealth with their children. The forefathers of this nation started out with bias, favoritism, nepotism, and a Eurocentric mind frame of an unfounded superiority complex from the beginning.

Not only were the natives of this great land called *merciless Indian savages* whose known rule of warfare is an *undistinguished destruction of all ages, sexes and conditions* in the Declaration of Independence, but the very same grievances that were being redressed by the forefathers of this nation to the king of England, which they felt were only being answered by *repeated injury*, were then and even now turned around and used against their own citizens, especially African-Americans.

Some of these grievances that are being redressed by African-Americans that come straight out of the Declaration of Independence word-for-word and are being repeatedly answered by injury or just straight altogether ignored are: the obstruction of the administration of justice for the black community; judges are partial in their judgments and have no sense of true justice, only what their own wills desire is their ruling; the government is constantly flooding our communities with new police officers to harass our people; and these same police officers are protected by the government when they violate the law by stealing, beating, and killing African-Americans with no regards for justice nor human life.

For decades now, these grievances have been trampled upon and not taken seriously. It's unfortunate that blacks have to physically act out, and people have to die in order to receive the attention that they have been seeking for the last 150 years in order to have their problems corrected.

When a people get used to being ignored and not taken seriously, they begin to expend much energy which starts as a *thought* first, and an action second into getting their points across, no matter what. Thus, all the predominant thoughts which are occupying space in their minds become thoughts of objective attainment. In the minds of most African-Americans, especially the ones who never could move up the economic/social ladder, the system (white America) is the great inhibitor which is always preventing them from *overcoming* and moving up the social ladder. This thought is so dominant in the African-American's thought pattern that it permeates his entire being and existence here in America.

The only way to remove these thoughts from the minds of African-Americans is to deal with the problems which caused these thoughts in the first place in a generational manner, for it will take time for blacks to unlearn all that they have learned for their protection from whites and their strategies for sustenance in this white dominated land. True *trust* takes time to establish. And considering the brutal history between whites and blacks here in America, the process of healing need to begin right now, for it may take longer than any of us has expected.

The Solution to the Problem (Black Side)

There is no one solution to the problem; there are many solutions. Each and every solution is one more piece to the grand puzzle which, in time, will manifest the *ultimate* solution. The *ultimate* solution is the *solution* to the problem. This solution will educate *and* empower the people on both sides of the color spectrum, and drag along everything in between on the path to unity.

Before we can deal with these solutions, we must first realize that there are those on all sides: black, white, brown, red, yellow, etc. who are predisposed to change, and no matter what anyone says or does to try to teach them or influence them to love those of the opposite race, they just aren't going to budge.

These people will have to be worked around and be overcame in the spirit of unconditional love, for they lack the spiritual understanding and the humanity of empathy which would create in them the desire to want to love and to share the human experience with all human beings regardless of their color, and ethnic or cultural differences. However, the process starts with the individual. Each individual person must step up and be accountable to every single person of the opposite race, and program themselves to no longer see race (i.e., black, white, brown, etc.) but only *equals*. After five years of this, the country will see immediate results in race relations.

Whites will have to stop being apathetic toward blacks and their plight. There is a kind of unspoken or unexpressed racism that most whites in America display in very subtle manners. For example, the mere thought that crime, poverty, and the disadvantage of illiteracy is exclusively a *black* problem. To most whites, it's opprobrious to be a black person in America. Until these innate predispositions about blacks are eradicated from the white's psyches, there can be no real progress, for it becomes almost instinctive for them to be biased toward blacks without justifiable cause. These feelings are then passed down from generation to generation without the generational successors ever even having a fair shot at experiencing blacks for themselves. It's programmed hate being preserved on an intergenerational level which leaves it extremely difficult to break the generational curse.

Blacks have to understand this generational conditioning by which whites are afflicted with, and not allow for it to dictate their feelings and actions toward whites. Once blacks and whites stop generalizing one another and start judging each person of the opposite race as an individual and by that individual's content of his or her heart, then there will be more room, more availability to allow for people of the opposite race to enter in into their lives, therefore removing the racial/social wall that had *no blacks allowed* written on it.

African-Americans, my brothers and sisters, we cannot continue to blame the white man, the system, America, the police, etc. for our conditions. It is what it is! I speak to you as a brother, guide, conscious leader, and newly erected pillar of the struggle. I now address you in our dialect of English. That way, everyone of all cultural and literacy levels of our race can understand my message.

We are our own solution! No longer can we wait on the white people of this land, the American government, or an invisible deity to mysteriously materialize from out of thin air and solve all of our problems for us. It was once acceptable in our culture to wait on GOD to deliver us while we just sit back and do nothing. For hundreds of years, we, as a people, have sat back and waited on Jesus to come and save us from all of our worldly problems while we have just sat around and done nothing but pray and believe. It's been almost 400 years now, and we are still doing the same old thing. Outside of the inhumane physicalities of the brutal institution of slavery, whether you all want to believe it or not, the truth is that we are actually worse off now as a people than we were in slavery.

Now, don't get me wrong. I, too, love the Lord, and I'm a very spiritual man. But we must realize, my brothers and sisters, that Jesus's kingdom is a *spiritual kingdom.* He dealt with problems in this world just like the rest of us even until it being the death of him, and GOD let him go through it. He asked Yahweh (GOD) two different times to save him, and Yahweh, in his divine wisdom, didn't. Everything about the whole Jesus experience was *spiritual,* so Yahweh, just as he does with us, uses physical experiences to express spiritual principles. Once the spiritual end is understood, then and only then does the physical suffering abate some, if not completely. Here is where we are with the African-American here in twenty-first century America. Our problem is a spiritual problem first, and a physical problem second. All of our problems here in America are spiritually based. Why do you think that GOD allowed for us to be taken away as African slaves and molded into so-called African-Americans anyway? *Spiritual disobedience results in physical suffering,* yet we pray and we pray but still do not understand the lessons which God afflicted us with, only for us to learn from and to return back to our pure natural state.

Faith without works is dead. Therefore, brothers and sisters who read as well as practice the teaching of the Bible, it is time for action. We must do our part, and *do* all that we can within our means to pull ourselves out of this drunken stupor that we have been in for the last 400 years

The reason I said that *we, as a people, were better off in slavery than we are now* is because, at least, when we were all slaves, we took advantage of the one thing that we all had in common (slavery), and although being from different tribes with different tongues from diverse parts of Africa, we still, while in the severest kind of captivity, managed to form a community out of ourselves even before we were called African-Americans, and we had each other's back one hundred percent, and rarely, if ever, murdered one another, unless we were forced to do so by our masters.

We shared what little we had, and we were always mindful of one another's issues with authentic empathy guiding our actions and responses. So I ask you all, my African-American brothers and sisters, *how could we go from a good sense of community and affinity for one another to a bad sense of individualism and hatred toward each other?* Let's keep it real, now!

For it isn't the white man or the police killing us, it's *us* killing *us*! We are twelve percent of the population in America, yet fifty-one percent of all murdered people in America are African-Americans. What's even more astonishing than this is the fact that ninety percent of all of the murdered African-Americans were murdered by other African Americans. That's us, my brothers and sisters! There is no entity or white person putting a gun to our heads and making us kill each other. We are our own problem and solution!

The three main things that we can do as African-Americans to receive instant results and begin to see the African-American world become what our ancestors and our one true GOD intended for it to be here in America are:

1. Acknowledge that we are one people with a unique history and relationship unlike any other group of people in America, and that we, no matter how hard we try to deny our spiritual heritage as Africans and replace it with secular philosophies and high sounding doctrines, "we are all we got!" We are GOD's chosen people regardless of what anyone may think or say about us or our condition. And as GOD's chosen punitively captive people, our salvation (answer to all of our problems) as a people is invested in us making amends to YAHWEH as a whole first, then using all of the abilities that the LORD has blessed us with individually as a cohesive whole, which will work to empower us enough to pull ourselves out of this bottomless pit of oppression and victimhood that has immobilized us ever since we first stepped foot upon this land of captivity and endured all of these centuries of unnecessary suffering;

2. Learn to love our self and our kind first before leaving our communities and attempting to love someone else of an unfamiliar culture. We have to become obligated and accountable to each other as brothers and sisters, and to our communities as a whole, as watchmen and life enhancers. Each individual among us who are able must be accountable to all those who are not. It has to become like a sin for any African-American who is able to see another African-American who is not, and then not help him become *able* himself.

The African-Americans' contribution to the U.S economy is over one trillion dollars a year. Thus, there is no excuse for not one African-American out of the entire forty-plus millions of us who live in these United States of America to ever not have everything that we need in order to be able to live productive, fulfilling, progressively enhancing lives here in this land which was made rich and built up by the blood and sweat of our ancestors.

If we love ourselves and we love our brothers like we love ourselves, then we wouldn't be as quick to offend our brother or to steal from him, try to harm him, cheat him, or do anything to his wife or any other one of his family members that would contradict love.

Once we have grown strong enough as a people to be able to love one another with each other's best interest, then we will be able to expand that love to those outside of the African-American experience whose energies are, more times than not, being directed toward the betterment and in the sustaining of their own communities and people.

The main thing is that we establish and maintain our own economic circle in our communities whereas every single person in our community, regardless of life choice or nonchalance, receive some type of benefit from our economic circle which will help to enhance their life. In learning to love each other, we will automatically learn to trust each other. In trusting each other, we will finally be able to not only overcome all of the disparities and disadvantages that has plagued us from our humble beginnings, but will also be able to finally start doing some *empire building*. So in just loving ourselves and loving each other, we will accomplish more than half of the solutions to our problems; and

3. The decisive issue that will determine our overcoming as a people will be our ability to finally be able to unite under one banner of solidarity, and get rid of all ideological and denominational barriers which have been erected by our oppressors to keep us divided and keep our resources scattered.

Ever since slavery ended here in America, there hasn't been one word that has had the kind of effect on African-Americans than the word *unity* has had. Whenever blacks hear the word *unity* concerning other blacks, most blacks cringe at the prospect of such a thing. The greatest illusion to ever hit black America, according to most blacks, is the illusion of *unity* among all blacks here in America. What we all have to realize, though, is the fact that without unity, we can't accomplish anything! Those who have sought to keep us inferior and of the lowest castes of society can only sustain this by keeping us divided. I assure you, my brothers and sisters, if we all unite under the party of DASP (The Descendants of African Slaves Party), and get rid of all of the denominational, ideological, philosophical, and religious barriers that separate us and prevent our efforts of uniting even before they start, there is nothing that we can't overcome or accomplish as a *united people*. But we must unite! There is no other way.

We can accomplish in five to ten years now what it would have taken our ancestors decades to accomplish in their times because we have social media and various other information highways that we can use to reach vast amounts of people now. There is no excuse for us as God's people to continue to be placed at the bottom of the barrel in everything that matters, when we ourselves right here and right now in this world at this very moment, have the means within our power to attain our end.   We are our solution to our problem! So let's solve it, my brothers and sisters.

White: A Brief History

Let me start off by acknowledging all of my white brothers and sisters, and letting you all know that I love you all and I'll never do or say anything about you all that's not commensurate with the truth. I am a learned man who was raised up and taught from a westernized Eurocentric perspective here in America for the first quarter of my life. For the next quarter of my life, I was taught and raised from a more universal perspective, even an Afrocentric perspective among others which most Eurocentric-minded people consider to be *inferior* in correlation to the Eurocentric perspective.

Thus, my perspective is universal, and it reflects all of the races and ethnicities of the world and all of the best things that their cultures, scholars, traditions, philosophers, etc. have to offer.

I don't believe in being biased, neither do I indulge in partiality. Everything that I'm about to write is the truth that I've been able to come up with after almost two decades' worth of research and study. Some people will be incredulous through their predispositions about information which comes from sources other than their own. However, I'll let the truth speak for itself as I break down these hard core facts which some have been deliberately suppressed by the dominant culture in order to not only control the propaganda machine, which works to maintain their imperial status quo of things and also to keep all those who would seek to exalt them, their way of life, and their culture to the almost divine-like status by which they have been conditioned to do in perpetual awe of them so that they can continue to dominate them and control them. With this being said, let us look at a brief history of the so-called white race.

The existence of white people, and especially white civilization, is relatively new in correlation to humanity as a whole. While white people make up only around ten percent of the total world population, such a thing as a *white person* or white human being didn't even come into existence until around 20,000 years ago.

It has been proven by science that the so-called white person here on earth has come into being as a result of copulation between Homo sapiens (blacks) and Neanderthals (whites). Prior to this happening, every human being on the face of the earth was a person of hue (color). Thus, the original hue-man (human) was a person of color (so-called *black person*).

Understanding and believing in such a truth, how could one be racist? The white race has always been located geographically in the same place where the Neanderthals were located—in *Europe*. Being cut off from the rest of the world during the last ice age, many distinctive genetic mutations and behavioral patterns were adapted by the whites. This caused for the now known as *Europeans* to not only look different from the rest of the peoples of the earth, but to also have different modes of behavior and a group ethos that was alien to the rest of the groups of the world which mostly had some type of dealing and interaction with one another. As I've written earlier in this book in chapter one, all of the mutations that had taken place with the first Europeans all the way down to their modern descendants, which are still a *recessive minority* on this planet, were all for the benefit of the survival of the newly formed mutated group which we now racially identify as white.

Even until this day, the highest percentage of Neanderthal genes that can be found in any group of human beings will be found in the highest percentages in those of European descent. Every person in the world that has had any intimate dealings with whites ever since their inception into the human family now has some percentage of Neanderthal genes in their genome. The only exception, which represents the only group of people on the earth today, that has zero percent of Neanderthal genes are people of indigenous African descent, which has had no intermingling period with the white race. This has come as a result of a lot of the African groups being so far away from the Euro/Asian interaction zones that they never had the opportunities to encounter the Neanderthal or white groups in order for the interactions to take place that would lead to the mating necessary for the genetic exchanges to occur between the species/races.

Whites, as a racial group, scurried around Europe/Eurasia for thousands of years before they finally founded their first civilization. The civilization of ancient Greece was the white race's (Europeans) first civilization. Established around 1400 BC, the Greek civilization was founded and built upon the remains of the splendid Cretan culture by which the then war-mongering barbarous Greeks had laid to ruins.

In between the time of the rise of the first white civilization and the twenty-first century where we presently are, there were many white empires to rise and to contribute to civilization. By far, the two greatest European empires which had the most influence over the way that the world is now were the Greek and the Roman Empires.

There is very little in the world, especially the western world, that doesn't have some form of Greek or Roman influence over it. From our politics to our customs to the very traditions that socially binds us together, European civilization has done a lot of good for the advancement of humanity. But it has done a lot of bad, also, mainly in world conquests by its idealistic conquerors and the reshaping of the world's geography. These two things alone can account for almost all of the problems which are going on anywhere on the face of the earth.

Whether it's imperialism, population displacements, or the superiority complex, it invokes the response of the dominant culture to interfere in every/any nation's business on the face of the earth and play the role of *policeman*. The western world, which are the inheritors of Greco-Roman civilization, is the standard of civilization in today's world. They represent what it means to be civilized, progressive, and the best of what humanity has to offer.

It wasn't always like this, though. Whites, like most other races, had several ethnic groups (tribes) which they descended from and were in constant strife with each other. Most of these tribes like the Gauls, Saxons, Jutes, Franks, Huns, Angles, Goths, Visigoths, Thracians, etc., were extremely hostile toward one another, and warred with one another continuously. One must remember that, unlike the rest of the known world then, Europe was still covered in ice and affected by the last ice age, so resources were scarce and the European population had to compete and fight for what little resources were available. While the rest of the world were establishing civilizations (i.e., Asia, Africa, Australia, the Americas), the Europeans lagged behind due to their hostile environment, warring factions, and a lack of resources by which to build upon. Being cut off from the rest of the world, trade was not an option for them. By the time that the whites ventured out of Europe, civilizations were already in full swing all across Asia and Africa where the Europeans would soon migrate to. This is where whites first started learning civilization. Then, after the Greeks thousands of years later, they put the finishing touches on this civilization's learning by learning from the Cretans before destroying their civilization and building upon it, the Greeks (Europeans/whites) now had a civilization of their own. They became master imitators, and sought knowledge and the latest innovations from all over the known world in order to further enhance their civilization. Once their civilization became solid, the conquests and imperialism began under the banner of *Hellenization*. Greek culture, by way of Alexander the Great more than anyone else, spread and dominated the then known world in such a way that history would still display the Grecian feats of the Greek Empire thousands of years later.

The next European successors of the Greek Empire was the Roman Empire led by ambitious leaders and generals like Publius Cornelius Scipio Africanus (circa 237 BC), Gnaeus Pompeius Magnus a.k.a. Pompey (circa 100 BC), Julius Caesar (circa 100 BC), and Marcus Antonius a.k.a. Mark Antony (circa 80 BC). The Romans picked up right where the Greeks left off. Conquering even more land than their Greek predecessors, the Romans conquered and Romanized every land in their path of conquest from the Britannia Island in the west to the Holy Land in the Middle East. They also, unlike their Greek predecessors, conquered a vast majority of Northern Africa, including Egypt and Mauritania.

After annexing all of the lands that they conquered to the Roman Empire, the Romans immediately Romanized everything about their new provinces, and forced the people to assimilate into Roman culture and accept Roman law as the ultimate law of the land.

The greatest thing that a person could have at that time was the privilege of being a Roman citizen. Anyone who wasn't a Roman or a civilized and esteemed Roman citizen was considered a barbarian (savage). Thus, everyone who wasn't an enemy of Rome and all things Roman sought more than anything else in the world to attain Roman citizenship.

If one only thinks about what's going on in the world today, especially here in America, they will see the same patterns being displayed that were displayed in both Greek and Roman conquests. American culture/civilization is the lone heir of Greco-Roman culture/civilization. One only has to look at our laws, political system, social system, government, word origins, monuments, value system, etc. Even our days of the week, months of the calendar, and titles of celestial bodies reflect the overpowering influence of Greco-Roman culture.

America embodies the best and the worst of the ancient Greco-Roman civilization. The main difference between America and the former, though, is that America was founded on a racist foundation. The United States of America was founded by white men, and was designed to be a nation for white people and by white people. Anyone else who wasn't white here in America were to be the burden bearers for the whites.

Europe, which barely had any natural resources as it is, had gone mad with castle building all over

Europe and had depleted over seventy-five percent of their tree population and was faced with an overpopulated continent with not enough resources to feed and to shelter all of its inhabitants.

Once the first European voyagers made it to the North American continent and saw how it was a land full of tall healthy trees, which stretched out as far as the eye could see, they instantly perceived that they had hit the jackpot. All of the European nations from small to great began to send their citizens and denizens alike over here in vast numbers in order to lay claim to some land in an attempt to reap wealth from it which would further work to enrich and empower their impoverished nations back in the European motherland.

After decimating the Native American population with warfare and disease, the Europeans needed an unprecedented number of laborers to help conquer this new wilderness called America (the New World). The solution to this problem was the African. In the African, the white man saw an unlimited supply of free labor, servitude, and capital. What would become of this new system of slavery in the process of nation building is the content and dilemma of this book. Let us dig deeper now!

The Making of the
White American

While we all know that it's true that all white Americans came to this land at one time or another from Europe or either descended from those that migrated here from Europe, it's easy to see that the now so-called white American, though of the same stock and motherland of the rest of the whites which are now scattered all throughout the world, are of a totally different ethos than the rest of their brethren are. No matter how far apart they may be, they still are brethren that are bound by the ties of consanguinity.

Most people don't realize that the first generations of Europeans to come to America were already of the lowest grade of European society. Countries like Spain, Portugal, Brittan, France, and the Netherlands sent their criminals, prostitutes, and all of the menaces of their society to America to colonize it and to claim land and wealth for their country of origin.

Europeans started emptying all of their prisons and mental institutions, and shipping all of their less desirables to America, Australia, South America, etc. to colonize and conquer the lands and the indigenous of the land in the name of the king or queen of their nation of origin. To refuse to do so, or to get to the new world and decide to do your own thing, would still be considered lèse-majesté and was punishable by death.

After years of the new world's lands being made habitable and safe by Europe's less desirables, the more aristocratic and prominent members of European society began to come over and to capitalize on the Native Americans, the less desirables, and all of the achievements of the less desirables.

These are your first *white Americans*. The literate whites were severely in the minority compared to their illiterate, uncultured counterparts. Nonetheless, both groups would, in time, end up being the masters of the African slaves which would be shipped into America in the hundreds of thousands and over the years end up becoming a new ethnicity called *African-Americans*.

It is an irrefutable truth that nowhere else in the entire western hemisphere was slaves treated worse than they were in America. Now, people can receive a better understanding why the institution of slavery in America was so brutal and so inhumane. It all started with the inhumanity of the individuals who would be called slave masters.

Their superiors, the people who sent them over here (even the private companies), knew about the pathologies and barbarous mentation of these first American colonialists/settlers. So once the brutality of slavery got underway here in America, every white all over the rest of the world including the pope turned a blind eye to the inhumane treatment of the African slaves who, in the view of most Europeans, weren't even fully human anyway. So empathy was an illusion in the minds of most whites when it came to understanding the black plight.

The Willie Lynch methods only worked to exacerbate the brutality of the African slaves, and further the trust gap between blacks and whites here in America. While whites in Europe evolved to a higher state of consciousness which invoked inside of them their higher sense of self and humanity, their American counterparts continued to devolve at an unfathomable pace to the point where their ethos as white Americans were far worse than the so-called barbaric black and native American savages who they sought to grind into the dirt in building their new nation for them.

Even white Europeans don't like or trust white Americans. Not only was the African-American created and molded in America by his experiences and history, but so was the white American slavery, conquest, white privilege, racism, nepotism, imperialism, barbarism, hypocrisy, lèse-majesté, and greed all are associated with the white American. Yet of these all, *racism* reigns supreme, does it not?

Racism in Society

Racism in American society here in the twenty-first century is so ingrained in American culture that even the immigrants who migrated here from all over the world experience it in some fashion or another, and end up picking up the spirit of racism themselves. There is no better example to illustrate this phenomenon than to use the group ethos of Latinos.

As you know, Latinos are a diverse group of different ethnicities and nationalities that share the same language and certain cultural values. In most of their lands of nativity, most of these groups don't even like each other. But once entering the United States of America and seeing how the society works over here, these same nationalistic ethnic groups, which had little or no dealings with one another due to ethnic differences when they were in their homelands, all of a sudden form new ethnic bands—a sort of Hispanic alliance where they become the proverbial *Latino*— and thus began to establish themselves in America as such, building their own communities (or moving into already established communities en masse in a move to become the dominant group/culture of that community) and keeping themselves Latinized and culturally sensitive to anything foreign, especially if it has to do with America's most historical undesirables—the African-Americans.

All of the world knows about the black man in America and all of the stereotypes that accompanies his reputation wherever it may be presented. American culture perpetuates these stereotypes through miseducation and misinformation by way of the greatest propaganda machine ever created—the media. The media, whether through radio, television, social media, newspapers, etc. consistently portray African-Americans to be lazy welfare recipients, gang members, aggressively bitter, angry, irresponsible, criminally minded, covetous, xenophobes, and extremely untrustworthy and dangerous to be around.

All immigrants, regardless of wherever they are emigrating from, have some kind of familiarity with this kind of propaganda concerning African-Americans alone. Thus, they enter the country with defenses up in preparation for the time when they will encounter the so-called brutish and uncultured African-American. They never really have a chance to experience an African-American or African-American culture themselves personally in order to make the evaluation themselves about the character or the idiosyncrasies of the African-American. Due to a history of and a well-developed system of systemic racism in American society, these immigrants receive an unwarranted predisposition about African-Americans before they even get here in America. So once here in America, is there any wonder that no racial group or ethnic group likes or trusts African-Americans?

There are many whites here in America who have been here forever, ever since they were born, yet they still haven't experienced African-Americans or African-American culture. I'm talking about people over fifty years old who have been in America that long but have never gotten to know any black people.

Also, I know many blacks who are over fifty years old and who haven't ever experienced white people. I can't say the same thing concerning white culture, though, for white culture being the dominant culture here in America, its influence over the lives of every single American is inescapable. It's an integral part of what it means to be American. Yet outside of the confines of this culture, most of the diverse races and ethnic groups don't really want anything to do with one another.

No one can argue the fact that our country is still mostly segregated. Albeit the segregation that exists now is individually voluntary instead of mostly legislative, it still exemplifies the disinclination of the various races and ethnic groups to want to physically interact with one another even under the banner of *one nation under God indivisible*, which is the summation of Americanism and what it means to be American.

Racism is an ingrained integral part of American culture whether we want to accept it or not. The truth is still the truth whether we believe it to be or not. Until we, as individuals, change the way we think and the way we perceive one another, there can never be any racial progress among the races here in America.

It's so bad in our country that even the institutional racism which exists inside of the church has been allowed to subsist for centuries now undisturbed. America's oldest and most sacred institution is undoubtedly the church. Did not a nice proportion of the Europeans that voluntarily migrated over here do so in an effort to flee religious persecution back home in Europe? So how can one flee persecution just to go and establish a system of persecution of their own? The hypocrisy of the founders of this country can no longer be ignored, neither can the inheritors of this nation from the founders (their descendants) continue to overlook the abuses of their ancestors and the effects of those abuses which are still having a negative impact on American society, as a whole, especially the African-American population.

GOD's church is supposed to be the pillar of society. The church/God sees no color, race, or creed. So why is it that the shepherds of His church/flock see these externalities that not even He sees in his divine omniscient state of being?

It's unacceptable for Christians to denounce other Christians because of the color of their skin, their political affiliations, or their cultural style of worship. Yet in this so-called Christian land of America, this is exactly what is going on. I've been in many churches in my life dealing with many different denominations. It's sad to say, but now I see why the terms *black church* and *white church* have found their way into the English vernacular, for such things exist in our society.

In totality, there are more racially segregated churches in America than there are integrated churches. The main reason for this is because *America is still segregated.* No one wants to admit it, but the facts are just too self-evident. Until we acknowledge this problem as a cohesive whole or as one group, we will never be able to dissolve this issue and efficiently integrate as a nation.

The differences in the black church and the white church reflect a bigger theme. Looking at these differences, one will immediately be able to see how wide the cultural divide is between black culture and white culture. Not only should such a thing not exist in a nation where you are supposed to be *one nation under GOD indivisible*, but regardless of what's going on in society or in the world as a whole, the church should never indulge in such divisive behaviors.

I understand that people are different and that different groups of people have certain group ethos and idiosyncrasies, however, the church experience is a spiritual experience more so than a physical one. Spirit has not color, shape, or mundane limitations. The same spirit of GOD that's inside of the black person is the same spirit of GOD that's inside of the white person. GOD doesn't see color or any of the other divisive tools or ideologies that man sees that causes him to separate himself from his brother or sister. Thus, the Christian is to see the world through the eyes of GOD, and respond to it accordingly. GOD is a god of diversity. If you believe in the GOD of the Bible, then you know that GOD receives all the glory of his creation. Thus, who are you to tell your god that "I'm sorry, God! I don't like the people with color on their skin that you created" or "I'm sorry, God! I don't like those people who look white because they don't have any color on their skin." This is asinine!

We, as human beings, have dug a pit so deep and so full of crap for ourselves that we can no longer move ourselves out of our own way in order to get out of the hole and forge a better future for ourselves. I'm so tired of hearing, "I don't like white churches because they don't preach right, praise right, or show emotion and love for the Lord during their services" or "I don't like black churches because they praise too aggressively, preach too aggressively, and are just altogether too wild for me."

Both sides, blacks and whites, aren't acting Christlike when they make such prejudiced statements about each other. God is spirit! All those that come to him must come to him in spirit and truth. So all of the other external inhibitors that we have erected for ourselves as a species have nothing to do with the love of God. I challenge all peoples of all faiths to show me your faith by your obedience. If you say and believe that Jesus is love, and that Christianity, Islam, and Judaism are religions of *peace*, then show me your obedience to the higher power and the holy book that you have placed all of your *faith* in because there isn't any love in racism, prejudice, nepotism, favoritism, exclusion, or anything else that divides instead of unites.

I must reflect on one more issue that reflects a more subtle form of racism in American society that many of my white brothers and sisters are very dismissive of.

There is such a thing as *white privilege,* and also the *privileged mind-set. White privilege* is what I like to call the *benefit of the doubt* factor. And the *privileged mind-set* is the conscious awareness of whites knowing that they have the benefit of the doubt factor to work with, and in worse case scenarios, even rely upon in severe situations that can end really badly for them. Look at it as kind of like extra lifelines, while everyone else who are nonwhite would be lucky if they got just one lifeline.

Some of the examples of white privilege which cannot just be written off as *ignorance by the hands of minorities* or as just simple coincidences as the percentage of minorities that are incarcerated here in America (especially African-Americans) in comparison to whites, who are the super majority of the American population, and the extant of the wealth gap which separates white Americans from all other Americans, especially African-Americans.

Did you know that in almost every crime category that exists here in these United States of America that whites get charged with the highest percentage of arrest than any other race in America, yet when it comes to the state and federal prison populations whites are only numbering in at around twenty percent? African-Americans alone, without adding any Hispanics to the equation, comprise of around fifty-four percent of the U.S prison population, and African-Americans are only 13.2 percent of the total U.S population which is approximately 350 million people now. How is it that far more whites are arrested for crimes than all other minorities? Yet minorities are the majority in prisons both state and federal all across America? We can't overlook what this is overtly conveying—*white privilege!*

I saw something very disturbing last year. There was this white kid aged nineteen who was found guilty of murder and was up for sentencing. Now, the white kid was small. He was around five feet four inches and weighed around 100 pounds. The judge, being an older white man, felt like the kid was too small to go to prison, so although the law required the kid to be sentenced to prison time for being duly convicted of the crime of first-degree murder, the judge reclassified the kid and sentenced him to house arrest and probation out of fear that if he sent the young white male to prison, he would be preyed upon by the predominate black prison population, and his conscience couldn't allow for him to do that.

Once this incident leaked out to the media, there was extreme backlash behind this judgment of the judge. After a little bit of investigating the judge's history on the bench, it was discovered that this very same judge had a history of being *tough on crime,* especially concerning black males. It was discovered that there were several instances where there were young and small black males who had even lesser charges than the white kid had, but were sentenced to almost draconian sentences by this very same judge. This brought the justice system all across America into the spotlight, and what was discovered in more states and jurisdictions than not was that such practices as the practice which was performed by the judge in order to spare the white kid from prison was the norm when there were white judges on the bench. This is a great example of *white privilege* and the *benefit of the doubt* factor that it invoke in others here in America.

White Americans are cognizant of their position in American society as being the dominant culture, and the descendants of the founders of this nation which now makes them the inheritors and preservers of America. This fact alone invokes the *privileged mind-set* inside of them and empowers them to feel entitled, for everything about America is built upon, molded around, and prophetically projected around white (European) culture dating all the way back to ancient Greece and everywhere else European in between. So anyone who doesn't think that there is a strong sense of pride with white Americans in dealing with American culture, there is something seriously wrong with them.

These facts that I am discussing are not abstruse by any means. It's just that such truths aren't inter-locutory in American society, but to the contrary are treated like taboos and are often brushed off when brought up, regardless of whatever the occasion or situation may be.

The wealth gap between black Americans and white Americans is directly related to slavery. It's an irrefutable fact that the poverty, crime, and wealth disparities that African-Americans are afflicted with here in America are due to the legacy of slavery here in America—245 years' worth of chattel slavery, to be exact. White privilege here in twenty-first century America even guarantees the fact that the poor white American will still have much, much more than the poor black American.

Structural advantages accrue to a wealth based white middle class over an income based black middle class. A wealth based white middle class has the advantage of being able to reproduce middle class status intergenerationally through gift or inheritance. Whereas the black middle class, being income based, is solely dependent upon the labor market to maintain status. Blacks own no real assets or have no real access to resources in order to attain real assets of value. While on the other hand, even if whites didn't have the structural advantage of the accrued wealth, white privilege alone would still grant them a very powerful alternative that black Americans could only dream of having, and that's the life-changing option of having the true access to the resources, which will work to help them attain the assets of high value which in turn would make them wealthy and wealth based anyway, instead of income/labor based.

Reparations can help African-Americans fill in the wealth gap some, but the gap over all these generations of single-sided wealth accruement by white Americans has increased exponentially. Thus, it is a strong likelihood that the wealth gap between blacks and whites may never be overcome. Speaking of reparations, why is it that white Americans almost instinctively cringe at the prospect of blacks (African-Americans) receiving monetary reparations from the U.S government for 245 years' worth of chattel slavery? Even if one asks for reparations just for the eighty-nine years of slavery under the established U.S government (from 1776 until 1865), people start getting shaken up.

The most popular statement that I hear from whites concerning reparations is: *Why should I have to pay blacks anything? I never enslaved anyone.* This statement by whites actually makes a good point. However, the nineteen trillion dollars U.S debt which was accrued over the last 150 years or so is a debt that is shared by all Americans, even African-Americans, who weren't even treated as Americans during the time that these debts were accruing. Yet and still, as Americans, they are required to pay their fair share of the debt whether they agree or not. So as America goes, so does her citizens. Thus, no one could really legitimately complain about reparations for African-Americans without actually feeling some kind of way about African-Americans personally, for blacks would be able to make the same argument about their share of the national debt due to most of the debt being accrued in wars that wasn't even in the best interest of African-Americans. We, as a nation, have to *keep it real* when it comes to discussing and dealing with reparations for African-Americans. For without white Americans aboard, the idea will never gain traction anyway, let alone be accomplished through congress.

Racism in American society isn't only unfair and unhealthy for its citizens of all diverse races, ethnicities, and nationalities, but it is also a hugely immoral wrong and a blatantly rebellious act against God/nature which is the primordial cause of all diversity which exists within our physical universe. It's like slapping God/nature in the face and saying, "You made a big mistake creating those white people" or "You made a mistake creating those black people." Being a racist is the ultimate expression of evil and ignorance among humanity. Society, as a whole, shall not and cannot tolerate this evil no longer. Whether we live peacefully and prosperously as a nation or be destroyed as a nation, it will ultimately be determined by our ability to get along as one people, as Americans, and not as black, white, Indian, Latino, Chinese, etc.

We need to rebuild our culture and make it a universal culture where everyone's ideas, concepts, and unique cultural contributions to society are all involved in the national standard of what it means and represents to be an American. This alone would immediately work to change the way that all groups of Americans see themselves, and in return, see their nation.

There would no longer be any special benefits in being *white in America*. We would finally have an *egalitarian* society. Let's keep it real, though. *Power succeeds nothing without struggle,* thus the benefits of being the dominant culture in a nation.

The Benefits of Being the Dominant Culture

There is nothing more empowering and inspiring than being around and being a part of a family, friends, supporters, and like-minded people who share the same values as you do. Such an environment is not only just a wholesome environment but is an environment where your likelihood of not succeeding in life in any manner of path that you put your mind to is almost unfathomable to even ponder.

This is what's going on in America today. As explained in the last chapter, white Americans are cognizant of their position in America as a white person. From birth until death, they are fed a diet of Eurocentric stimuli that are designed to build them up with a sense of confidence, entitlement, race consciousness, and pride that will empower them to think as leaders and the vanguard of American culture (which is synonymous with European/white culture) and the inheritors of the nation itself.

This ideology is reinforced by the dominance of American culture/society by the pervasive overexposure of white propaganda and Eurocentric curriculum. It's almost naïve to not think about white supremacy when looking at America as a whole. According to Webster's New World College Dictionary, *white supremacy* is defined as "the social, economic, and political repression and exploitation of nonwhite peoples, especially blacks, by white people, based on notions of racial superiority."

Being real with ourselves, we have to admit that the founding fathers of this nation, according to Webster's definition of white supremacy, were *white supremacists*. I know that using the term white supremacist in the same sentence as *founding fathers of the United States of America* will rattle a few people's emotions, and maybe even enrage others. However, as I stated earlier, "I am not a divisive person, but a person who believes in being united!" Due to our historic past as a nation, though, whites tend to get really sensitive and perturbed when the truth comes out euphemistically about the racial part of American history. If we can't deal with each other, or at a minimum, tolerate each other in light of the truth, then everything that we are all working toward in relation to race relations in this nation is all for nothing, for we will never be able to fully trust one another enough to be able to let our guards down for a minute and step out in faith in our efforts to embrace and to learn to understand and to love those of our brothers and sisters of the opposite race.

Thus, it's vital that we not deal in pride, and instead deal in truth, regardless of whatever shape or form it manifests itself in truth, my brothers and sisters! *Truth!* It's all about the truth! To confirm the racist intentions (white supremacy) of the founding fathers of this nation, one only has to look at the fact that *blacks weren't even considered human beings by the founding fathers, but instead, were valued as chattel.*

As a matter of fact, the constitution of the United States of America, thus Americans, didn't even recognize blacks as people until 1868 under the Fourteenth Amendment of the United States Constitution. So if you repeal the Fourteenth Amendment, blacks, according to the U.S Constitution, will no longer be considered human—only three-fifths of human—and thus have "no rights by which a white man has to respect"—in the famous words of former chief justice of the United States Roger B. Taney (served from 1836–64).

The purpose of blacks was to be the burden bearers of this nation. They, as human beings let alone as U.S citizens, were not part of the founding fathers' vision for America. Slavery, by which most of the founding fathers and early presidents indulged themselves in by owning many slaves, was the sole purpose for the black people. So anything that is going on today, which works to do anything for blacks outside of keeping them as inferior servants (slaves), is working against the constitutional spirit of slavery and the prophetic destiny for blacks in America which was visualized by the founding fathers of this nation. As I stated earlier, all immigrants who migrated to these United States of America buy into the whole *suppress the black people ideology* once they arrive here like all other non-blacks here.

For those of you who isn't familiar with this or isn't familiar with the dynamics by which African-American communities all across America operate, just look at the economics in just about every single predominantly black community in America. The first thing that will stand out to you is that well over 50 percent of all businesses in the black community are owned by non-African-Americans. To be more specific, they are owned mostly by the Arabs, Chinese, Koreans, and whites. Hispanics are known to own a number of stores in the black community also, but not in the numbers that all of the above-mentioned groups do.

Reverse the situation now and let's look at the mentioned communities of the racial groups I described above. What one will immediately realize is that none of the communities mentioned above will have even a ten percent African-American economic presence in their communities. No one wants to be bothered with African-Americans because they don't trust African-Americans. Nonetheless, they all desire to tap into the African-Americans' consumer spending, though.

Nowadays, most blacks are aware of these behavioral patterns being displayed toward them by the other races. Yet in the mind of most blacks, they think "if I could just somehow become more white American-like, I can then receive some of the benefits myself of being white in America. For then, white people will know that I'm one of them, and then they will trust me enough to give me opportunities that people of my race don't normally get here in America."

White supremacy dictates that all nonwhites acknowledge white people as the founders and pre-servers of civilization, the standard par excellence for all things signifying success and royalty, and as the rulers of the world by which all other races and ethnic groups must abdicate their inalienable rights to in order to be able to exist and to have a productive livelihood here on Earth. By whites owning the vast majority of wealth and resources in the world, the benefits of being the dominant culture are limitless for whites. All other nonwhites must assimilate into white culture, and play the game of white supremacy with an ethnical hand of playing cards that doesn't possess any aces or kings in it. Thus, unlike whites, these groups have to do that which is unnatural to them, mainly behave and think white mindedly and always simultaneously keep their minds centered upon the fact that they aren't nor ever will be *white*. All whites have to do is just do what comes *naturally* to them; that is—*be white.*

Being the dominant culture and the standard for everything *great*. Whites have most of the world for-saking the traditions, norms, and cultural expressions of their ancestors in order to become *whitewashed* so they can be acceptable to those of the dominant culture which now influences not just the western world but the eastern world, also.

People are going as far as lightening their skin, straightening their hair, dyeing their hair colors like blond, red, and brown, and becoming unhealthily skinny in attempts to try to become more into the image and likeness of whites in order to be more acceptable to them. When people do these, they are constantly reinforcing the *European standard of beauty.*

It has gone so far now that most races, especially the men of the races, will have nothing to do with the women of their own races if they aren't in possession of the abovementioned European features, although such features are uncommon among the members of these races. People's natural physiognomy and anatomical group traits are being dismissed as ugly and inferior, and are being replaced with more foreign European features which are deemed to be more attractive and even more prurient in most cases.

Western/European civilization has dominated the entire world and has placed economic, political, social, geographical, and ethical standards upon all of humanity that has consumed the planet and ushered in a *new world order* without anyone even noticing.

To be white and to be a part of this new world order is more than just simply beneficial, it's life shaping. However, for all nonwhites, it's like a cat and mouse game trying to keep up with the joneses, while at the same time perpetually working to build a solid foundation for their posterity.

Once there is no more such thing as the *dominant culture* but only culture, uniting as Americans will become that much easier. We cannot forget, though, that there are those who are so reprobated that nothing in the world will or can dissuade them from their ways of hate, dissension, racism, and their white supremacist superiority complexes.

We cannot allow for the likes of such people to inhibit our progress at uniting and building a better America for our children. No longer can a culture or a people be *dominated* by another culture or people. Until we, as a species, master the art of *equality*, thoughts of power will continue to mesmerize us and blind us into doing its bidding of expanding itself. To expand itself, *power* has to dominate. We can no longer be slaves of power. But now, let us all be slaves of *love*. That way, there will be "benefits as a human being in one culture" instead of benefits given and shared by the "dominated culture;" which is keeping America separated and divided.

The Predominant White Thought About Black People and America

The predominate white thought about black people is ostensible. It is, the thought of blacks as being aggressive, criminally minded, angry, lazy, dependent, and untrustworthy.

The predominate white thought about America is the thought of America being the land of the free, the land of their ancestors, the land of plenty, their land of divine providence, and the greatest country in the history of mankind. The predominant white thought about black people, and the predominant white thought about America are in complete contrast to one another. This difference in the thought process of whites is one of the main psychological conflicts of interest which influences them to deal with blacks the way that they do. This is also why it is so easy for whites to stay away from blacks, and to remain apathetic about blacks and their plight here in America. For to deal with the blacks is to have to deal with their unsavory culture and white threatening idiosyncrasies. Then, there is this other influential thought inside of the minds of whites which most people rather leave unnoticed. This is the thought of fear of retribution by the hands of blacks for all of the bad they have done to them over the last 500 years. This thought was manifested on an international level when President Barack Obama was running for the presidency in the year 2008.

A lot of white TV personalities were joking around a lot and saying things like "Hey, Obama! If I vote for you and you win, are you going to enslave the white race for what they've done to blacks?" I also heard numerous amounts of white voters (mainly older white voters) say straight out of their own mouth, "I just can't bring myself to ever vote for a black person." Some went as far to even say "Who's to say that this black man Barack Obama who's running for president won't try to enslave the entire white race if he wins the presidency and becomes the leader of the most powerful country in human history?"

People like these and statements like these were all over the radio and television during the 2007/2008 election season. What rattled me the most, though, was the fact that no one on any of the news networks were calling these old racists out on the words which were being spewed out of their mouths. That was a perfect time period for many teachable moments in race relations in this country. Yet everyone was doing the same thing they've been doing for the last 400 years in this country when whites verbally or physically abuse blacks, they *look the other way* and move on with their lives.

Whites in positions of power here in America all know the unwritten rule of *watch the blacks and keep their minds monitored at all times.* All educated whites, though not knowing how to deal with it, know the history of America and the perpetually unstable relationship that exists between America/white people and blacks. Feigning ignorance has become the white Americans' trump card in addressing and dealing with race relations in this country. This is the main reason why this problem has been allowed to persist for so long.

Those people that I spoke about in the last chapter that are so "reprobated and are full of hate, dissension, racism, etc." mostly are older white people whose dispositions toward blacks are so far gone that it's all but useless to even try to open up their eyes and teach them how to love blacks. The only thing that stays on white people's minds are self-preservation, the American dream, and maintaining the status quo. By whites perceiving blacks as destructive to American civilization, they rather not have anything to do with them at all, especially allowing for them to share their communities and social structures with them. So the most common way that even the so-called *nonracist* whites deal with the racial issue with blacks here in America is by denial. Not to mention the fact that by keeping themselves isolated from blacks and black problems, they never have to deal with race issues anyway. This keeps them in further denial.

They figure that as long as they can keep the blacks away, race doesn't have to be a part of their world anyway. But as soon as the blacks come around or either they themselves find themselves in a position where they have to be around blacks, then their *race consciousness* kicks into play.

Whites can be very condescending when dealing with nonwhites. This haughtiness is reinforced by the culture being molded and formed in a way that reflects back to all nonwhites the image and domination of whiteness.

All whites aren't racist or self-centered. White people are part of the human family, regardless of their impact upon the world or the hatred that most of the world has for them and their form of civilization.

White Americans, for the most part, are very patriotic and love their country dearly and will die before they will allow for anyone or anything to destroy it. We, as Americans, have to learn how to understand one another to the point where we can tolerate one another's differences out of love rather than hate for each other or out of fear.

It is vital that we all learn how to control our thoughts, and define for ourselves what our dominant thoughts should be and not allow for society or culture to do so. For if we can't live in and control that little area of space that only we ourselves occupy which houses the brain, then how can we lead and guide someone else into the light (truth)?

My white brothers and sisters, this is how you all can implement your part of the solution into the equation and help us all do away with the racism which has consumed us and fed off of us as a nation for the last 400 years. We need you! This is what is required of every single white person in America to do in order for us to end racism in America.

The Solution to the Problem (White Side)

What you all can do right now immediately to have an instant impact on the race relations with blacks in this country is to first get it into your mind that all blacks don't hate whites, or are all criminals. This alone will help whites to start the process of learning how to see blacks differently, individually, and thus start opening up a little bit by giving themselves a chance to get to know blacks and to understand them. *Understanding* cannot be underestimated. Almost all of our problems as human beings stem from some form of misunderstanding. Being the dominant culture and the standard for the *true American*, whites are in a great position to help effect real change.

Everyone knows the history of slavery and its legacy. Though being a horrendous history, the races still have managed to coexist over all these years without wiping out one another. This confirms the fact that there is hope between the races. Whites must step outside of their comfort zones for a minute and reach out to blacks, seeking to ingratiate a friendship with them. I assure you that most blacks will respectfully embrace this gesture, and more times than not, a fruitful friendship will result.

Whites also need to train blacks for better paying jobs, and open up the resource lines to blacks so that blacks can have more opportunities and more resources to take advantage of the opportunities that they receive. Now don't get me wrong, it's not like African-Americans can't do everything for themselves that need to be done in order to liberate themselves from the yokes of mental slavery and economic poverty. African-Americans are very able to accomplish such feats. However, with the help of white people, it will be much more attainable with much more efficiency.

White Americans, especially those who are in influential positions, know that if they wanted to really get something done or changed in this country, they could do it very easily for they have the money, power, and the resources to ensure that whatever it is that they need done will be done.

White people can play a major role in helping blacks by helping to get laws passed that will give African-Americans all the extra opportunities that are afforded to white people instinctively through white privilege.

Understanding that black people are extremely higher to commit crimes or to fail at achieving success in America than whites because of the circumstances that are surrounding Blacks (i.e., poverty, crime ridden environments, single parent households, low literacy levels, etc.), whites need to set up a system through legislation where the penalties for African-Americans are more reformative than penal.

Black culture is a unique culture that was formed under sui generis circumstances. It has both all the good and all the bad of American culture/civilization intertwined. Looking at black culture in all honesty, though, one will see many disturbing idiosyncrasies that have evolved with the culture from slavery until now. Such things as parents beating their kids with branches off of trees, eating the intestines of pigs, the darker half of the race not trusting the lighter half, strong dislike for the plantation overseers (police), and fatherless households all have evolved and assimilated into modern day African-American culture.

Whites can no longer portray to be nonchalant about the black plight. The best thing that whites can do to be a part of the *solution* and not the problem is to "make themselves available to African-Americans when needed, and allow for their resources to become African-American resources temporarily for the sole purpose of the African-American developing the necessary means to become self-sufficient and self-reliant."

This is just as good as *reparations* if appropriated right. Think about this and the other suggestions that I have suggested to you, my white brothers and sisters. To agree is to make progress in race relations in this country. I encourage you all to *do the right thing*.

A Comprehensive Conclusion

Ignis fatuus will not be the case with this all-inclusive movement to end racism here in America. Unlike movements of the past, ours is one that is perpetual and progressive, ever gaining more momentum as we accelerate punctiliously toward our goal of unification and true amalgamation.

All of us—every single individual—must play the part of amalgamator in order for us to succeed where all of our predecessors have failed.

The twelve things that must be done in order for us to end racism in America are:

1. *Every single person need to reach out to people of the opposite race and seek to understand them, their ways of life, and the content of their heart.*

Children should be guided into these experiences also by their parents, seeing that the survival of any people relies on the education of its young. We must program our children and teach them altruism while they are still young, before society and media get a hold of them and start conditioning them toward stereotypes and predispositions of the opposite race.

2.   *America has to acknowledge its wrongs done to black people, who are now known as African-Americans, through the North American slave trade.*

By acknowledging its wrongs and apologizing to African-Americans, who are now the descendants of those African slaves who were brought to these American shores in shackles, for slavery and its ugly legacy which still affect African-Americans even today. America will be sending a powerful message to African-Americans that true repentance does still exist in government, and that true repentance calls for true forgiveness by African-Americans. For until blacks and whites can get past the whole *slavery* situation, there can never be full peace and amiability between the races. History has proven this time and time again.

3.   *There has to be a constitutional convention that is reflective of twenty-first century America, and not eighteenth century America.*

The demographics of this nation has shifted irreversibly. For the first time ever in the history of this nation, whites are about to be a minority in the nation that they founded for white people and by white people. Laws need to be legislated, which reflects all Americans regardless of their: sexual preferences, life choices, race, color, creed, religious affiliations etc., for racism cannot end until there are only Americans in America. As long as there are African-Americans, Native Americans, Mexican Americans, German Americans, English Americans, or even white Americans, there will always be conflict, for humans are a proud species with large egos. Each group, although American, will continue to hold on to the national heritage of their ancestors, and most, if not all, will be German, English, or Mexican first, and American second just like their ethnic identifications signify (i.e., Mexican-American, German-American, English-American, etc.) This within itself is and always will be a problem in this country if it isn't done away with strictly American nationalism.

Johann Friedrich Blumenbach did more harm than good when he used the term *race* in 1775, to classify the diversity of man. And for a token to all of his readers, he displayed his superiority complex by coining the term *Caucasian* which alludes to the racial supremacy of whites. According to Johann Blumenbach, "the Caucasian race is the most advanced and superior race among mankind." (Read Johann Friedrich Blumenbach's *On the Natural Variety of Mankind*.) Racial pride is not only illusive, but it's offensive and divisive. This cannot go on in America if we are to end racism. We must come to terms with the fact that there is only one race—*the human race*. Quick as we can embrace this truth, the quicker we can end racism here in America. It's literally just that simple!

4. *There has to be some form of reparations for African-Americans.*

According to Webster's New World College Dictionary 4th Edition, the word *reparations* means "a repairing or being repaired; restoration to good condition. A making of amends; making up for a wrong or injury."

I know we discussed reparations earlier, however, it's become the one subject that most Americans (mostly white Americans) do not want to talk about. I've already explained in previous chapters why reparations are needed. Now, I will dig deeper into how the reparations should be applied in improving the African-American condition here in America.

First of all, I know that a large portion of whites who are for reparations are against *monetary* reparations. However, some form of monetary reparations will have to be given to African-Americans in order for to achieve the results that we seek to achieve by granting African-Americans reparations in the first place. There has to be a *money loop* developed in African-American communities so that they can learn to be self-sufficient and self-reliant.

Until America becomes the nation of Americans, the ethnic/racial signification of *African* will always precede the American in African-American, thus African-Americans still have to look out for African-

Americans, for history has shown us that no one else will.

Monetarily, every single African-American should receive $50,000. Those who aren't eighteen years old yet shall receive their $50,000 on their eighteenth birthday. That way, you don't have young African-American kids growing up saying "I didn't get any reparations" because their parents or guardians squandered it. And for all future African-Americans who are not yet born during the paying out of the reparations, the responsibility of quality of life for those individuals will be solely upon their parents, for they would have had an ample opportunity to engage in capitalism, and thus secure the future of their offspring.

The second phase of the reparations for African-Americans shall consist of building them institutions—hospitals, schools, mental institutions, banks, etc. If you noticed, I have not mentioned *land* yet, though land is the most valuable aspect of reparations that African-Americans can receive (especially land with natural resources). The United States of America is one of the most, if not the most *land greedy and land selfish* nation on the Earth! So to ask for land and to really expect to receive it, especially here in the continental U.S, is a real long shot. But GOD's word says, "You have not because you ask not." Therefore, we are asking in his name. However, it is only right that African-Americans take a shot at this long shot since their ancestors' blood and sweat filled and built this land which was once wilderness and overtaken by trees.

America has options that can be exercised to accommodate the African-Americans' request. There are islands and territories that belong to the U.S that can be given to African-Americans if the U.S chose to do so. Nonetheless, the African-Americans' main aim is land here in the continental U.S where they have slaved and lived ever since 1620.

The Nation of Islam's minister Louis Farrakhan tried to get the U.S government to grant him land in the U.S Northwest so that he could develop a nation for African-Americans. President Muammar al-Qaddafi of Libya was in support of Farrakhan and offered to give Farrakhan two billion dollars to help establish the would-be new nation for African-Americans. The United States denied Farrakhan the land and denied him the two billion dollars from Qaddafi, saying that Qaddafi was involved in terrorism, thus his money couldn't enter into the U.S for no purpose whatsoever.

Farrakhan had a great idea; he just was in the wrong time dealing with the wrong nation. He even wanted to take all of the African-Americans who were incarcerated with him. Releasing African-Americans who are incarcerated as a part of reparations is another necessary part of the reparations appropriations.

There is no doubt that the vast majority of African-Americans who are incarcerated in state and federal prisons in this country are incarcerated there in some form or fashion as a result of the legacy of slavery.

In between biased legislation by the hands of racist legislators, inequalities in the educational and work fields directed toward blacks, and the creation and containment of blacks in highly volatile, high risk communities now known as ghettos, it's all but impossible to be a black man growing up in the ghetto and not ever experience jail or prison.

As mentioned earlier, *slavery created these conditions* and white power has sustained them—very methodically, I may add! No education, resources, real ownership, or voice to be heard and acknowledged by those in power that has the means to make a difference in black communities equals frustration, which equals aggression, and we all know what aggression leads to—*violence!* Violence leads to prison or death. Everything is interconnected; it was designed this way. It's almost as if blacks are deemed less threatening to whites when they are held captive in controlled environments. Nonetheless, blacks are suffering and are perishing in what is supposed to be the most liberal and freely expressive nation on earth. Yet black lives in America are constantly regulated with dreadful regulations and behavioral modification like legislation. It's by design, and it's always been by design. But now it must stop!

America can save itself billions of dollars a year, and rid itself of its fearless less desirables if it gave African-Americans land outside of the continental U.S, and send all of its African-American prisoners there also as their reparation appropriation from the U.S government.

This last idea actually isn't unheard of nor should it be hard to accomplish, seeing that this country was founded by such European exiles, and so was Australia.

Thus, in giving African-Americans reparations for the crime of slavery and racial oppression, the United States will not only be repairing a wrong that was done to a people over a span of 350 years on their soil under their jurisdiction by their founding fathers, but they will also make peace with the children of their original sin—the descendants of African slaves—and thus, open up the door for real negotiation and advancements in ending racism here in America.

5.   *The entire educational system and curriculums need to be reformed.*

The educational system here in America and all of its curriculums are outdated and still have very high white supremacist over tones all throughout. Instead of brainwashing kids with the likes of Columbus discovering America, civilization starting in Greece, *our* forefathers founding America, pre-American Africans and native Americans were savages before being civilized by whites, etc., kids should be educated in practical education instead of classical education. Kids should be taught how to till the soil, how to make medicines and preventive herbs for ailments, and how to *know thyself* for in knowing *thyself* one will not only be able to know and to understand others, but also they will intuitively become self-reliant and self-sufficient.

What good is it to know about Socrates, Queen Isabella of Spain, Christopher Columbus, George Washington, European history and culture, etc. if I can't get a job or don't know how to survive off the land? It's like, to be acceptable by whites in America, one must learn to conform to European thinking and behavior. Carter G. Woodson in the *Miseducation of the Negro* said, "The same educational process which inspires and stimulates the oppressor with the thought he is everything and has accomplished everything worthwhile, depresses and crushes at the same time the spark of genius in the Negro by making him feel that his race does not amount to much and never will measure up to the standard of other peoples. The negro thus educated is a hopeless liability to the race." Education has to become more practical and also more reflective of twenty-first century America with all of its diversity.

People must learn how to differentiate between indoctrination and education. Indoctrination has produced the *herd conformity* which has dominated American culture and has made the masses weak and powerless. Herd conformity is learning to accept uncritically the pronouncements of authority and to buy truth as others see it without engaging in our own thinking. Education, at minimum, not only has to be practical but has to be life-changing and life-inspiring. Teachers need to start being held to the ancient African standard of *if the student doesn't surpass the teacher, then the teacher is considered a failure.* This ensures that the teacher gives his all in teaching his students, and also that the student is actually progressing. It also does away with westernized quota systems which doesn't work at all. We need an educational system that brings out the best of the individual, and is then applied to his or her life practically. This is how society and civilization will evolve!

6.   *Conflict management must be instilled in every single child.*

Conflict is inevitable in this world whether it is with our family, friends, or with strangers. Conflict cannot be avoided. The decisive issue is how we respond to the conflict. Many lives both old and young have been destroyed by instinctive violent reactions to nonviolent situations. I know our history as Americans is full of violence and rebellion. It's a part of the American spirit! But in today's times with the weaponry that's available to do damage to people, this American war spirit of times past is doing more harm than good. It is vital that we, as a nation, learn how to resolve our conflicts without using violence. This discipline has to start with the young. And for to be sure that our children are being brought up right in dealing with conflicts, a *conflict management* curriculum should be developed and taught to children as early as preschool. This would ensure that the child's mind is being properly developed in a *nonviolent* fashion regardless of whether or not the child's parents are doing their job in teaching the child conflict management.

7. *Xenophobia must be done away with.*

Xenophobia is a word that is unknown to a lot of people, but what most people doesn't know is that *xenophobia* is one of the key factors behind racism and also unwarranted dislike of foreigners. Xenophobia derives from the Greek words *xenos* meaning "foreign or stranger," and the word *phobos* meaning "fear of." So the word xenophobia means fear or hatred of strangers or foreigners, or of anything foreign or strange. This is singlehandedly how racism started in the world in the first place. Neanderthals were afraid of Homo sapiens, and Homo sapiens were afraid of Neanderthals. Whites were afraid of blacks, by whom white people considered to be *unruly and savage*. And blacks were afraid of whites, whom black people considered to be *ghostly and sickly*. This sense of xenophobia isn't just limited to the races. Pretty much any encounter that has ever happened between man and beast, man and innovation, or even man and phenomena has resulted in xenophobia in their first encounter. But after developing an understanding concerning things, man usually loses the xenophobia. The fear of the unknown no longer has its effect on man at that point.

Today in the world, man is more stubborn than in his entire history. He hates without cause, distrusts for reasons unfounded, and he fears any and everything that isn't a part of his group or circle. In America, the scene for this type of xenophobia is overexaggerated due to the melting pot that is America. This makes it so much easier for xenophobia to translate over into hate and physical reactions due to the close proximity of the various races and ethnic groups.

Unless *xenophobia* is done away with, it is *impossible*, and I mean literally impossible for racism to end here in America, let alone on Earth.

My solution to end xenophobia here in America is to as usual, *start with the young first*, then work upward creating a new mental culture and bringing about awareness to all Americans concerning the *universal collective consciousness* that we all share together.

Once people begin to realize that we are all the same, and that the only thing that is different about us is our external variations, people will begin to realize their folly in xenophobia, racism, nepotism, etc., and will start accepting everyone unconditionally and love them because of their humanity and not the lack of.

8. *A new culture for African-Americans must be established,*

I love my African-American brothers and sisters and everything, but the truth is the truth. In the condition that we are currently in, it is all but impossible to make peace with America and with whites like this. You all know why I am saying this, my brothers and sisters. We don't even love and respect ourselves, let alone someone else.

It is time that we unlearn everything that we have learned over our 396 years of captivity that has worked to divide us and program us to engage in self-hate. Until we love one another and respect one another, how can we authentically demand this conduct from the white Americans, Hispanics, or Asians who capitalize off of our community, and then at the end of each day, return back to their own?

I encourage all African-Americans regardless of color, class, religious affiliation, or political association to start preparing themselves mentally and spiritually for a recreation of African-American culture that is very much needed.

Once we change the way that we see ourselves, then the way that we see others will change, also. When we change the way that we think and the way that we see and engage the world (especially America) as African-Americans, our culture will begin to change automatically. What's left to be done after the renewing of our minds will only be to express our newfound selves in light of our new minds. This will be our new culture where every day will be a new day to add on to and to express our culture. It will be perfected as we live it pragmatically. Then and only then can we authentically demand respect from others.

9.   Race camps should be built for race offenders.

I choose not to use the term *racist* but instead *race offenders*. You see, a racist and a race offender are not the same thing. Though the race camps would be built for the housing of both groups, they are not one and the same. A *racist* is a person who believes in the superiority of one race over another, or a person who feels hatred, bigotry, or prejudice toward someone because of their race. A *race offender* is a person who jokes, jest, or unintentionally does or says things to the opposite race or races that could be taken as offensive by that race, although the race offender said it or did it without the intent to offend.

One may ask, if the person's intent was all in jest, then what is he doing wrong? I'll tell you what's wrong with this situation and why we can no longer tolerate it. Pending our history in this country and its very violent, racist beginnings, most people, even if they portray to be otherwise, are racially sensitive. This applies to both sides of the racial dividing line in this nation.

It's become common over the years for both blacks and whites to socialize using racial overtones and speaking condescending racial epithets to one another all in so-called *jest*.

The problem with this, which has been irresponsibly overlooked all these years, is the fact what was said best by Jesus Christ, "Whatever is in your heart determines what you will say" (Luke 6:45).

Thus, for such things to come out of someone's mouth reflects the content of their hearts. This doesn't necessarily make them racist because they aren't doing these things to prove superiority over someone else or to even try to hurt that person. They are only doing these things out of their conditioned state of expressing themselves as true Americans—both the good and the bad characteristics of the American ethos all enveloped inside of one individual. They ignorantly and unwittingly offend without knowing they are offending. And the victims on the receiving end of these offenses, though offended internally, externally displays a conditioned façade as if not to offend the offender who is the initiator of the whole situation. In the end, both spiritually and mentally, no one wins. Such common daily occurrences as these are only exacerbating the racial problem here in America, and they need to be halted immediately.

Race camps would be a closed, controlled environment where racists and race offenders all dwell together, mingled in with superbly altruistic individuals who loves them unconditionally and who choose to express this love for them by overcoming their hate with love and by teaching them through practical deed rather than through word of mouth that we are all the same and there is no reason to fear or hate.

All people in the camp would learn how to overcome their racial insensitivities and learn to become *mindful* of others, even when those others aren't even mindful of themselves.

Race camps are a key component to optimizing race relations in this country. After leaving the race camps, racists and race offenders would have spent good quality time around the opposite race, and would then have personal experience under their belt in dealing with all people. Thus, they will learn how to judge people by the content of their heart and not the color of their skin.

10. *The president of the United States needs to establish a permanent department to deal with race relations and racial matters specifically.*

This should have been done a long time ago in this nation, seeing that four million newly emancipated African/African-American slaves were set free and unleashed upon society with no education, property, or formal assimilation into white American society. We have to also consider the fact that most white Americans (especially in the South where the slavers were) already felt that blacks were only three-fifths of a man whose sole purpose of being was to serve the white man and to cater to his every need.

These whites became enraged and very offended when the U.S Constitution gave the once chattel slaves equality with the white Americans, and insisted to white Americans that blacks were now protected by the law. That current generations and the vast majority of their descendants which have persisted throughout time even until this present generation have had nothing but contempt for blacks. They camouflage it under all types of confederate sympathizer groups which they justify their doings by claiming *heritage* instead of racism.

There has to be a mediator/stabilizer, preferably a governmental entity, to perpetually govern the affairs of race relations in this country. Though I'm not a *big government* type of guy, there are times when departments and sub-departments are necessary in order to focus on specifically targeted areas of distress dealing with the nation's issues whether they be people, places, or things.

The Department of Race Relations in America (DRRA) is needed, and should be established sooner rather than later. This is a prerequisite if we are to finally end racism in America. The same government that sanctioned slavery here in the U.S must be the same government to correct its former wrongs and end it.

11. *GOD must be in the center of everything.*

Despite the decline of religion in America and the increase of GOD bashing across all social spectrums, no one can underestimate the fact that GOD is still a part of American culture, and is still the strength of the American fabric which has made the United States of America the most prosperous nation in the history of mankind.

It is novelettish to not bring up nor incorporate GOD into the problem-solving nexus which shall work to do away with our race problems in this nation.

There is no disrespect to all of my fellow Americans who don't believe in GOD. I am here to unite and not to divide! Please, never forget this! Those of us who do believe in GOD still love you all as if you all believed in GOD, also. However, our perspectives will continue to be much different than yours due to our spiritual values. Standards that define our lives as followers of GOD. This doesn't make us any better than you all in any form or fashion. All this means is that our thoughts and our actions are conditioned and stem from an unseen force which is faith based, instead of corporeal senses based. Thus, there should be no dividing factors in this difference.

This nation was founded on the *GOD factor* by the founders of this nation. Regardless of some of their ideological gaffs, they did believe strongly in GOD. They knew just like I know that if God is ever removed from civilization, civilization will die instantly. The only thing that separates the *haves from the have nots* is the GOD factor. The GOD factor is the only real behavior regulator for the poor. For, the poor wouldn't be content with being poor if you removed the spirit of contentment which comes from GOD out of the equation.

Without all of the inhibitors by which religion enforces upon its adherents in place, the religiously preoccupied poor would then, with no inhibitors stopping them from doing whatever their minds conceived of doing, would just take everything that they wanted/needed from those who possessed it. It's the fear and consequence of GOD rather than men which controls the mind and spirit of the poor. It's quite the opposite when it comes to the rich. Eight out of every ten blacks believe in GOD in comparison to five out of ten whites. Thus, the powers that be in this nation, which are predominantly white, have to learn how to communicate to the masses (especially African-Americans and Hispanics) through the language of GOD which is spirituality and not religion per se. Also, no more can the *masses* be punished for the corruption of those they cannot restrain. As long as racism is keeping the people divided in this country, the powers that be can continue to rule and steal that which belongs to the people without ever being questioned.

The economic consequences that will trickle down to the people from the corruption of the *higher ups* will, and what is mostly known, to, create further tensions between the masses. They will vent their frustrations on each other—blacks blaming whites, and whites blaming blacks—when all along, it is the *powers that be* that are responsible for the conditions of the masses. GOD must be in the center of everything, especially the relationship between blacks and whites in America. There should be a nationally televised symbolic marriage between blacks and whites wherein you have blacks and whites of all ages and all walks of life come together at an appointed place. A huge appointed place, I may add, and make vows before GOD vowing to love each other through thick or thin, bad or worse, good or great, rich or poor, and through all of life's vicissitudes no matter what the future may hold for them. After hugging each other and kissing each other to finalize the vows before GOD, every black person shall place a black ring on the white person's right ring finger, and every white person shall place a white ring on the black person's right ring finger.

These gestures with the rings will not only be sanctioned by GOD and man as to be a symbolic gesture between the union (oneness) of blacks and whites in America, but will also work to create a *consciousness* among all Americans and among blacks and whites all over the world that *we are one species in the Lord!*

Worldwide, everyone will start displaying their black rings and their white rings as signets of the covenant between them, God, and the opposite race. Sooner than you know, *it will be cool to love and be with blacks, and it will be cool to love and be with whites.* Past racism and racists will become obsolete. Humanity will begin their new journey as one people and as one hope. Starting here in the most racist country on earth first, and then spreading all abroad to all lands and peoples in the name of love, hope, and unity! Without GOD, however, all will be impossible. Let us not let go of GOD!

12. *The truth must be taught.*

My brothers and sisters of humanity, I can't state enough how important it is that we start telling the *truth* to one another. The government and those who are in power got there and they remain there by feeding us a diet of lies. They get away with it all the time because we are so used to being lied to that we can no longer differentiate a lie from the truth even in dealing with each other among our own social groups and communities.

How can you trust someone who would, for one truth, tell ninety-nine lies? This is exactly what we are getting from *Big Brother*, though. They tell us what they want us to know, and that's only the thing to keep our minds occupied while they rob us, steal from us, and infringe upon our rights right in our faces with our eyes wide open.

They want us to continue to have eyes, yet not be able to see. They want us to have ears, but not be able to hear or even understand any of the aristocratic machinations they are devising in order to keep the rich richer and the poor poorer spoken all in their sacred languages of greed and legalese.

No more can we accept lies from our government, social institutions, religious leaders, family members, or even ourselves. Until we learn how to deal in truth with ourselves and with one another, nothing that we do or build will stand, for a foundation of lies isn't even strong enough to build a cotton house on top of it, let alone a covenant of universal love enveloping all of humanity in its nucleus.

Each law that is passed is an amendment of the social contract. For it to be valid, the parties to the contract must have assented to it.

Remember, my brothers and sisters, *the government and the people that run the government works for us!* They only have as much power as we give to them. So please stop thinking that the government's in charge! You are in in charge! We are in charge! We the people! Conquerors can't be trusted to truly educate the conquered. So whenever you have a conquered people who have been brainwashed and lied to into believing that they weren't conquered but saved from themselves by the same people that conquered them only to find out that they've been misled the entire time and subjugated by their oppressors for mischievous aims, there's going to be big problems and trust issues.

This is what is going on in the minds of African-Americans who are quickly waking out of the drunken stupor of ignorance that has plagued them over the last 400 years. Most blacks see the government and white people synonymously as the oppressor/conqueror. This is another hurdle from the black side of the track which will have to be overcome by blacks in order to be able to allow themselves to learn how to love and trust white people/America.

Both learned and unlearned whites and blacks know the truth that a vast majority of African-Americans doesn't like America and what America stands for. The foundation behind these feelings are based solely on the history of slavery and its legacy. So it is important that whites must understand African-Americans and their side of the story and learn to deal with them in truth, regardless of what that truth may say or do.

The truth is what it is! It speaks for itself, and it doesn't need any help proving itself.

Let us teach the truth, speak the truth, and live the truth unceasingly! Trust will result from this. And from trust, we shall find love, unity, and the beauty of humanity which reside inside of all of us indiscriminately. We must teach truth!

Theses twelve steps to unify us all and do away with racism in America are *guaranteed* to work if we apply them correctly with the authentic desire to achieve change and unity among the races in our country. I know this book isn't the absolute answer to our race issues here in America. Nonetheless, it's a start—a great start at that. This is the *beginning of the end of racism in America!* We all must do our part now to exact the results that will change our nation forever. It begins right here and right now, my brothers and sisters. The fate of this country is in our hands. Let us do more and say less! May we succeed at achieving our life and nation saving goal! Peace and love be upon you all!

Last Word

Although much wasn't discussed about Latinos (Hispanics) in this book, I felt it is only right to acknowledge our Latino brothers and sisters and to speak upon the so-called problem in America between African-Americans and Latinos. I found no better contemporary source to define what's going on between these two ethnic groups than a chapter out of the book entitled *The DASP Q and A* written by Richard Sharp Jr. a.k.a. El Khulil Hanoke DASPU. It's very informative, and I know that it will enhance your understanding of the relationship between African-Americans and Latinos exponentially. Thanks again for reading *Black, White, and the Beginning of the End of Racism in America.* I encourage you to get involved and do your part personally to contribute to the ending of racism in America.

Peace and blessings be upon you!

From the authors Richard Sharp Jr. and Elaine Sharp.

From the DASP Q and A…

Is there a problem between African-Americans and Latinos?

It has always bewildered me how ignorance can turn a person against his or her own self, causing him to dislike himself, even to the point of detestation. What is a Latino? Is a Latino some sort of other species from the line of Homo or something? Surely not! So why do people view so-called Latinos as another branch of human beings or some entirely different race?

A vast majority of Latinos possess some amount of African blood inside of them, thus making them no different biologically than African-Americans or any other black that fell victim to the great *diaspora*.

The only thing that separates so-called *Latinos* from the rest of us children of Africa is their culture and language, which they have been indoctrinated with since first being brought to the West Indies and the Spanish Americas.

There are those white Latinos, too, that have no modern African blood pumping through their veins like the majority of their black Latino brothers and sisters do. It is predominantly this group of Latinos who are *race conscious*, and in some instances, even racist against blacks—so-called African-Americans— and even colored Latinos of all ethnic backgrounds that they feel that they are superior, too, due to their white heritage and biological physiognomy. I have dealt with many of these whites, and I have seen firsthand the way they treat the ethnic Latinos. I have even personally investigated this so-called *beef* between Latinos and African-Americans. I have put over twelve years' worth of research into this investigation. These are the facts that I have come up with: first of all, a majority of both African-Americans and Latinos are ignorant when it comes to knowing and understanding anthropology, sociology, biology, and history which are all important and significant to know in order to fully be able to understand themselves and each other, thus the root to any so-called problem, hatred, or beef which were developed.

Not just Latinos, but many other ethnic groups and peoples who have migrated to the United States have found something very distasteful about African-Americans.

Most immigrants and descendants of immigrants find African-Americans to be haughty, arrogant, and brutish in their dealings with other human beings, even themselves. This perception creates a kind of *closed spirit* within the souls of those people, and guides them to dislike the African-Americans and view him with a strong dislike, which in the end, becomes a strong generalization and all-consuming stereotype toward the entire race.

African-Americans, once cognizant of the negative energy that's directed toward them via these other races and ethnic groups, then becomes even more belligerent and snobbish. Thus, the never-ending struggle of the pendulum begins, and it continues until acted upon by an outside force.

The day is coming soon, though, when the Latinos will be the majority in this country and will have more power than they have ever had in this country. Then people's true colors will begin to show, so will their true intentions.

Race pride will be displayed even more fervently than it was during the black 1960s here in America. Only this time, it will be the Latinos doing the showcasing, and their numbers will be many. Even the *black* Latinos among them will forget their blackness, and will embrace their Latin heritage and exalt it to the same degree by which they exalt their god. Hostilities with African-Americans at this point will reach a climax, and there will be blood.

Let all of the temples of DASP that's erected at the time of these happenings that I've mentioned above be known as *peace centers,* which will work to reconcile the differences between our people and our beloved so-called *Latino* brothers and sisters. We are one people! We share the same blood! Culture and systemic indoctrination are minuscule and are to be shunned for higher values.

There is no longer black, African-American, Latino, Hispanic, etc. when it comes to us, it's only the *Daspians!* for we are all that remains of our African ancestors who were forcefully brought to this hemisphere in chains.

Regardless of the traces of white or native American blood that also run through our veins with our African blood, we are still predominantly African, and we are undisputedly *descendants of African slaves* also known as Daspians. So why bicker and have strife with one another over customs, traditions, and indoctrinated cultural values? We are all Daspians! All of us! Let all of us love each other as such, and work hard to prepare a more peaceful and prosperous future for our progeny.

DASP!

Note to the Reader

All quotes and statistics used in this book, unless otherwise noted in the chapter, can be found in the 2015 Almanac or on the Internet.

About the Authors

Elaine Sharp is a mother of five who has been on both sides of the tracks of violence. She lost one at the age of thirteen, Joshua Sharp, from violent crime, and one at the age of nineteen from *Theory of Accountability*. She has twenty-one grandchildren and three great grandchildren, soon to be four. She received her Associate of Arts in 2001, her BA in sociology in 2003 (made the National Dean's Book), and her Master of Social Work (MSW) in 2006. She began that journey at age forty-six and finished it at fifty-one to set an example for her children, grandchildren, great grandchildren, and community. All *glory* to GOD who is the head of her life.

Richard Sharp Jr. is the founder of DASP (the Descendants of African Slaves Party) and is a true autodidact in every sense of the word. He was born and raised in the Roseland community on the Southside of Chicago by his two loving and conscious parents, Elaine Sharp, by which he authored this book with, and his beloved father, Richard Sharp Sr.

As a youth, Richard showed extraordinary skills in the sciences, and in the ability to lead and to organize. He has done much community work in the area of conflict resolution and lifesaving, as he was able to prevent many inner city youth from self-destruction, and helped to get many homeless boys and girls off the streets and into schools/houses of refuge-159-the house he was born and raised in with his parents and grandparents; who fostered many children and adults with a home of "unconditional love."

Today, Richard is a full-time leader of the struggle for equality for African-Americans in America, and a leading body in the struggle for race relations.

www.ingramcontent.com/pod-product-compliance
Lightning Source LLC
Chambersburg PA
CBHW070128260726
48658CB00001B/305